CREATING HER EMPIRE

DISCOVERING A WOMAN'S PURPOSE

21 INSPIRING WOMEN SHARE THEIR STORIES OF TRIUMPH

**MAELI NELSON & SANDRA HOLLADY
WITH 19 INSPIRING WOMEN**

© 2024 ALL RIGHTS RESERVED. Designed, Edited & Formatted by Everyday Woman, LLC - Self Published by Everyday Woman Publishing in collaboration with Everyday Woman Co-Authors within this book. To learn more, contact everydaywomanco@gmail.com

No part of this book may be reproduced or transmitted in any form whatsoever, electronic, or mechanical, including photocopying, recording, or by any informational storage or retrieval system without the expressed written, dated and signed permission from the publisher and coauthors.

LIMITS OF LIABILITY / DISCLAIMER OF WARRANTY:
The co-authors and publisher of this book have used their best efforts in preparing this material. While every attempt has been made to verify information provided in this book, neither the co-authors nor the publisher assumes any responsibility for any errors, omissions or inaccuracies.

Contents

CHAPTER ONE
From Religious Cult to Empire
by Maeli Nelson...5

CHAPTER TWO
Rebuilding After the Storm
by Sandra Holladay...13

CHAPTER THREE
Like a Phoenix Rising
by Jennifer Wright...22

CHAPTER FOUR
What the Heck? Oh! I Get It Now
by Tamra Wright..29

CHAPTER FIVE
Courage & Kindness to Ourselves
by Michelle Torres...36

CHAPTER SIX
Conquer Yourself
by Shay Stone..42

CHAPTER SEVEN
Free to BE All of Me
by Emily South...50

CHAPTER EIGHT
Purpose is In Your Presence
by Amandha Zhane..59

CHAPTER NINE
Trust, Luck, and Elbow Grease
by Katie Jo Finai..66

CHAPTER TEN
Live Your Dream Life Now
by Jasmine Nesbitt...74

CHAPTER ELEVEN
It Takes Grit
by Christina Haws..80

CHAPTER TWELVE
The Ray of Sunshine Rekindled
by Samantha Woodward 87

CHAPTER THIRTEEN
Weathering Storms
by Noa Bel 94

CHAPTER FOURTEEN
Courage Beyond Borders: A Path To Freedom
by Vivienne Pierre..102

CHAPTER FIFTEEN
Monetizing Your Passions: The Two Golden Circles
by Sunny Purcell..109

CHAPTER SIXTEEN
Inhale Truth, Exhale Trust, Embrace Change
by Pamela Kushlan 116

CHAPTER SEVENTEEN
The Unstoppable Journey: Manifesting Your Path
by Alexa Shaw 124

CHAPTER EIGHTEEN
My Journey of Strength and Forgiveness
by Brianna Magarrell 132

CHAPTER NINETEEN
The Woven Threads of Life
by Rossina Lake...139

CHAPTER TWENTY
Your Empire Within
by Nathalie Herrey...146

CHAPTER TWENTY-ONE
Embracing Change: Redefining Success After a Setback
by Angie Hewett 153

Introduction

Dear Reader,

As you embark on this journey through 21 beautiful stories, prepare to be captivated by women who have unearthed their true purpose in life. These narratives are not here simply to impress you but to impress *upon* you the unwavering truth that no matter where you find yourself in life's tapestry, you possess the power to rewrite your story.

You are not bound by circumstance. Within you lies the strength to heal, transform, and seize the reins of your destiny. Right now, in this very moment, you hold the key to unlocking your goals and fulfilling your life's purpose.

With excitement bubbling within our hearts, I invite you to delve into these tales of triumph, allowing their radiant energy to ignite the spark of your own purpose. May these stories serve as a guiding light, illuminating the path toward a life overflowing with meaning and fulfillment.

Embrace the power that resides within you. Your empire awaits.

We invite you to join our extraordinary community of women who, every day, make bold sacrifices to unlock their true potential and build their empires as business owners and real estate professionals.

History has shown us that no self-made millionaire achieved success in isolation. To rise to our fullest potential, we must surround ourselves with those who understand the relentless drive to make a difference in the world. We must stand shoulder to shoulder with those who understand the unique challenges faced by women in business. Together, we can create a powerful force for change, empowering each other to achieve greatness.

Take the first step and join our movement today.

With Love

Sandra Holladay and Maeli Nelson

https://www.facebook.com/groups/749824642330097

CHAPTER ONE

Maeli Nelson

Maeli Real Estate (Flippin With Mitch And Maeli)

Co-CEO

https://linktr.ee/maelinelson

Maeli's journey is a living testament that you can redefine your limitations. Raised in a restrictive cult where her purpose was cooking, cleaning, and childbearing, her mother's escape at 11 became a spark of enlightenment. Stepping into a classroom for the first time at age 12 ignited a lifelong thirst for knowledge. This transformed Maeli's world, unleashing a burning desire to empower herself and others.

Now a mother of two, Maeli's success is a testament to defying expectations. Married to her soulmate and business partner, her mission extends far beyond herself. Driven by a desire to leave a meaningful, lasting legacy, she's on a quest to empower 10,000 women to break free from the cycle of financial struggle and achieve generational wealth.

As an international speaker, top real estate agent, and investor, Maeli's impact is undeniable. Her diverse portfolio exceeding $17 million and a track record of over 250 successful "fix and flips" speak volumes. Yet, her true passion lies in guiding others. Through her show "Flipping with Mitch and Maeli," she showcases the journeys of her real estate students, illuminating the path to financial independence.

Maeli's message is clear: join her community of fearless investors and unlock your own potential for financial freedom. Together, you can transform your life and achieve greatness.

From Religious Cult to Empire

By Maeli Nelson

This chapter isn't just about my story; it's about showing you, the reader, that no matter where you come from or what challenges you face, you can find your purpose and build something incredible. It might not be easy, but it's absolutely possible.

In the realm of human existence, where intricate narratives intertwine like threads in a tapestry, my story serves as a beacon of hope, a testament to the transformative power of perseverance. It is not merely a chronicle of personal triumphs and tribulations but an invitation for you, dear reader, to embark on a journey of self-discovery and empowerment.

Regardless of your socioeconomic background or the obstacles that may have shaped your path, know that within you lies the potential for greatness. It is through adversity that character is forged, and true purpose is revealed. While the journey may be arduous and fraught with challenges and setbacks, it is a path worth treading.

Imagine a canvas, blank and pristine, awaiting the artistry of your own hand. With each stroke of the brush, each layer of color and texture, a masterpiece emerges, reflecting the essence of your unique soul. Your story, like a work of art, is a testament to your resilience, your creativity, and the limitless possibilities that lie within you.

Embrace the challenges that come your way, for they are the crucible that transforms ordinary clay into extraordinary porcelain. Through perseverance, you will discover hidden strengths, cultivate resilience, and develop a deep spring well of inner wisdom. It is in the darkest of nights that the stars shine brightest, illuminating the path forward.

Remember, you are not alone on this journey. There are countless others who have faced similar trials and tribulations and have emerged victorious. These stories that you are about to read serve as a source of inspiration and a reminder that with determination and unwavering belief in yourself, anything is possible! So, dear reader, let a glimpse inside each of our stories be a catalyst for your own transformation. Embrace life's challenges, for they are the raw materials from which greatness is forged. Believe in your potential, for it is infinite. And know that with every step you take, you are creating a legacy that will endure for generations to come.

Hitting Rock Bottom: A Catalyst for Change

For years, I flourished as a star salesperson in the cutthroat door-to-door industry. It was a demanding profession that pushed me to my limits, but it also brought me a profound sense of accomplishment and financial security. The thrill of closing deals and the camaraderie with my colleagues kept me energized and driven. However, fate had a cruel twist in store for me.

One seemingly insignificant misstep during a training session with a new hire drastically altered the course of my life. I suffered a debilitating injury that left my left leg paralyzed, and I was confined to a wheelchair for nine arduous months. The medical community was perplexed. Doctors offered no clear diagnosis or glimmer of hope for recovery. Their blunt words rang in my ears – the possibility of never walking again, of never fulfilling my dream of teaching my young daughter to dance, weighed heavily upon my heart.

During those dark days, despair threatened to consume me. The vibrant, active life I once knew seemed like a distant memory. My sense of purpose and identity were shattered. The future stretched before me as a bleak or uncertain landscape.

Those nine months were the darkest of my life. The pain was unrelenting, and the career I'd built was suddenly out of reach. With two young children (ages 4 and 7) depending on me, the weight of responsibility felt crushing. I felt lost, questioning everything – was this all there was? Had I wasted years of my life only to lose it all?

As my world continued to turn grayer and grayer, more medical bills kept stacking up. The amount of over $120,000 – an impossible mountain of debt – for a surgery that did finally fix me. But now I have to learn to live with the burden that the cost of walking again was going to be losing our house. I watched my children pack their favorite toys into boxes, too young to understand the weight of what we were losing. Each box felt like another piece of myself chipping away. Was every dream I'd held for them, for myself, going to crumble like this? Yes, yes, it was. We humbly moved back to Utah from Temecula, California, and moved in with family. With really nothing but suitcases, our dog, and our two kids. This stress ripped apart our beautiful family, and my husband of 10 years now has a painful memory.

Rising from the Ashes: A New Beginning

But a strange sense of clarity emerged as I hit rock bottom. My mother, who had bravely left a religious cult to give me a chance at a different life, wouldn't have endured such hardship for me to simply give up. I owed it to her, my children, and myself to create a better life. A deep conviction washed over me – this wasn't the end, but a turning point.

With renewed determination, I prayed for guidance. I knew events in our lives happen for a reason, but I desperately needed a sign, something to show me *why* this was happening. The very next morning, as I tearfully drove my kids to school, a seemingly random real estate investor trainee sign caught my eye. This sign was yellow and had the ugliest handwriting on it - it screamed "unprofessional"! But something inside me said to call.

I'd always loved the idea of real estate investing but assumed I needed significant savings to get started. Now, that dream felt laughable. Yet, desperation propelled me to dial the number.

In that transformative moment, a single act of courage unlocked a world of possibilities. The workshop I attended was a revelation, presenting stories of people from diverse backgrounds who had achieved remarkable financial success through real estate, often without substantial capital or credit. A surge of hope filled me as I realized this could be my path, too.

The workshop introduced me to a proven system, the concept of passive income through rental properties, and the accessibility of education at minimal cost. It ignited a newfound purpose within me: to embark on a journey of real estate investing, helping others escape financial hardship.

This path aligned perfectly with my existing strengths. I have always had a deep love for people and a knack for problem-solving. Leveraging these skills, I dove headfirst into the world of real estate, determined to make a positive impact.

Seven years fast forward, I found myself in a beautiful paradox. The journey that began with a courageous leap of faith led me to my soulmate, my mentor, my business partner, and my best friend – all rolled into one extraordinary person, Mitch Nelson. Together, we embarked on a mission to empower others through the five pillars of wealth. Self-development, business, banking, taxes, and real estate Investing. We established a thriving business, sharing the proven system that had transformed our lives with countless aspiring investors. It has been an incredibly fulfilling journey, witnessing individuals from all walks of life achieve financial freedom and create a lasting legacy for themselves and their families.

The path we chose is not without its challenges, but the rewards have been immeasurable. The single act of courage that opened a new world has led to a life filled with purpose, passion, and the joy of making a meaningful difference.

The 3 Pillars of My Transformation

The journey from despair to building an empire wasn't easy, but these principles became my guiding light, and I believe they can be for you, too:

- **Be Grateful:** Challenges became opportunities for growth. My trials instilled empathy, making me relatable and better equipped to help others.
- **Be Coachable:** No matter your experience, a coach provides perspective and accelerates success. We all get stuck; a coach helps navigate those roadblocks.
- **Find Your D.R.I.V.E.:** This powerful system helped me pinpoint my true purpose the "why" behind my every action. **What's Your D.R.I.V.E.?**

How do you unlock your full potential? How do you revolutionize your relationships? How do you exponentially increase your success? **The DRIVE system customizes these answers for you!** There is a reason our conversations fall flat. We are not speaking the right language. There are five core traits that DRIVE successful interactions: Directors, Relators, Intellectuals, Validators, and Executives. You connect with people based on your own DRIVE, which means you may not effectively reach the other 80%. The good news is that with DRIVE, you have the potential to master the other four languages and increase your positive results by 400%. Embracing these principles, I found the strength to rebuild my life. Today, I have financial security and freedom and the deep satisfaction of helping others find their own paths to success.

Your Journey Begins Now

You, too, have the power to create your own empire, a life of purpose and legacy. Don't let your circumstances define you. Embrace gratitude, seek guidance, and ignite the fire within. You deserve to live a life filled with joy and impact. I'm here to support you on this journey. Take the D.R.I.V.E. test in my bio section, and let's connect!

CHAPTER TWO

Sandra Holladay

501K Commercial

Acquisition Consultant

https://linktr.ee/sandraholladay
https://www.instagram.com/sandraholladay
https://www.facebook.com/realestatebysandra
https://www.tiktok.com/@sandraholladay

Sandra Holladay is an extraordinary entrepreneur, real estate agent and investor who has overcome significant challenges to achieve success. Despite facing divorce and starting over in her later years, she has remained resilient and determined.

Sandra's journey includes running an in-home daycare, venturing into real estate, and designing two 9000-square-foot homes. She also obtained a real estate license and co-founded Utah WREIN Creating Her Empire, a network dedicated to empowering women in real estate.

As a commercial Acquisition Consultant, Sandra has established herself as an influential force in the industry. Her passion, creativity, and unwavering commitment consistently yield outstanding results, solidifying her as a highly valued professional in the real estate world.

Rebuilding After the Storm

◆

By Sandra Holladay

In the tapestry of life, resilience is the thread that stitches together the fabric of our experiences, weaving tales of triumph from the threads of adversity. This chapter narrates a journey of fortitude that traverses the valleys of trial and ascends the peaks of empowerment, overcoming obstacles, embracing change, and discovering the power within. My life has shaped me into a woman continually creating and recreating her "empire" through resilience and a commitment to dreams. It's a testament to the power of women to navigate life's twists and turns, emerging stronger. I'm grateful for the lessons I've learned. If we don't experience adversity, we cannot fully appreciate the joys. I firmly believe that within each of us lies the power to overcome obstacles and forge a path to success. It's not about avoiding failure altogether; rather, it's about persisting despite setbacks, which has ultimately shaped me into a stronger individual and enriched my life in unimaginable ways.

I spent nearly 3 decades building a life in my marriage, sharing the joys and challenges. We weathered financial storms and infertility. I was diagnosed with type 1 diabetes at the age of 12, which compounded the infertility issues we faced. I have always had amazing support from my family, who taught me to look at the positive side of life. I've learned to pick myself up and start over, stronger, better, and wiser than before. From experiencing infertility came the profound joy of adoption. Despite nine years of trying to conceive, I persevered through miscarriages to finally experience the miracle of two full-term pregnancies. I cherished the opportunity to be a stay-at-home mom and raise our 3 amazing children. I established an in-home daycare to maintain this commitment until my husband's career flourished and alleviated financial pressures. Sacrificing my career to prioritize our family allowed me the invaluable opportunity to nurture our children while my husband pursued his professional goals. I cherish those years' memories, recognizing motherhood's profound impact.

Together, we embarked on the journey of building our dream home, engaging in the design and contracting process, which I found immensely gratifying. With a background in interior design, my passion for construction and architecture, inspired by my father, fueled my enthusiasm for this project. It was one of the most rewarding adventures I had pursued. I envisioned teaming with my husband to plan and develop neighborhoods once he had firmly established his career and our children were older. This ambition has been a lifelong dream.

After residing in Idaho, Utah, and then to Georgia, where we raised our family, purchased our first home, invested in real estate, remodeled homes, finished homes, lived in and rented out homes, purchased a business, and eventually built our dream home, we embarked on a new business venture that took us to Beijing, China, for a year. Our 2 daughters joined us while our son served a mission in Washington state. While our time in China provided us with memorable experiences, meaningful connections, and education in a new country and culture, our daughters ultimately desired to return to their schooling in Georgia, prompting our journey back.

Life took an unexpected turn with divorce and tested my resolve and resilience over two years of legal proceedings. It was the most heart-wrenching chapter of my life, leaving me awash in feelings of betrayal, doubt, inadequacy, hurt, and a sense of failure. While divorce was painful, it became a catalyst for profound self-discovery. Through this transition, I've unearthed my true aspirations and passions. I had dedicated myself to our home and community, leveraging our resources to uplift others, hosting gatherings, and volunteering extensively; my days were filled with enriching connections and meaningful contributions.

Amidst this challenging time, I decided to let go of our cherished dream home to embrace a new beginning. Despite the daunting circumstances, this experience fueled my determination to pave a brighter path for my children, and I secured a home for us to move to. After the divorce was final, we contemplated the possibility of relocating across the country. I decided to put our house on the market despite the unfavorable economy. Surprisingly, it sold within a day, at $25,000 more than I purchased it for the year prior. This was a clear sign, guiding us to the west, specifically Utah, where unforeseen opportunities awaited.

Assisted by the support of friends and family, I relocated across the country. This was a monumental endeavor for me. As my children acclimated to their new surroundings, attending school and securing employment, I pursued and obtained my real estate license, opening the door to a world of possibilities. Drawing upon my passion for home design and staging, I obtained certification in home staging and launched my own staging business, which brought me immense fulfillment. While I thoroughly enjoyed collaborating with builders on staging new homes, I recognized the greater financial potential in real estate sales. I shifted my focus to home sales while continuing to offer staging services to clients preparing to list their houses.

In the ensuing years, we experienced moments of profound joy and heart-wrenching sorrow. My three children celebrated weddings within a mere 10 months of each other, prompting us to shuttle back and forth between Utah and Georgia to plan and carry out wedding festivities. Shortly after these joyous occasions, our family was struck by profound loss. My father's passing due to a stroke led us to gather for funerals in both Georgia and Idaho. A year later, tragedy struck again as we bid a sad farewell to my brother, also from a stroke, and we traveled to Colorado to honor his memory. It was a period marked by three weddings and two funerals, encompassing a range of emotions and experiences that shaped our families' journey.

Amidst the twists and turns of life, unexpected opportunities emerged, and I embraced a new adventure to work with a local furniture and design store. I assisted clients within the store and in the comfort of their homes, providing personalized design solutions tailored to their unique preferences and lifestyles. I loved the opportunity, but I was still selling real estate, and the demands of retail hours often conflicted with my desire to spend time with family. Balancing the demands of work and personal life became increasingly challenging, prompting me to reassess my priorities and explore alternate avenues for professional fulfillment.

I had enjoyed investing in the past with my spouse and now desired to educate myself and venture out into the investing world again. With a passion for learning more about different investing platforms, I journeyed to deepen my knowledge and create a supportive community. After attending an enriching online investing course, I felt compelled to start a local group for women interested in investing. Bringing together 25 like-minded women from Utah on Facebook, our venture began around a table at Kneaders Bakery and Cafe. We began hosting monthly events with expert speakers, fostering learning and connection. The group continued to grow, and we formed some lucrative relationships.

As our group blossomed, I orchestrated a dynamic panel featuring seven remarkable women, each a luminary in her respective field: from a savvy woman contractor to astute owners of vacation rentals, insightful mortgage lenders, and adept fix and flippers. The event was a resounding success. Driven to elevate our gatherings further, I sought accomplished women to grace our monthly events, including my now esteemed co-administrator. What began as a speaking engagement swiftly evolved into a pivotal partnership, propelling our group's growth trajectory. Witnessing our community burgeon from its modest origins of 25 members to now boasting nearly 700 individuals, fostering a supportive environment where powerhouse women began forging paths to success together.

Through our group, I've been fortunate to encounter remarkable women and establish meaningful bonds. One such encounter led me to a woman involved in off-market commercial investments whose fascinating projects piqued my interest. I extended an invitation for her to showcase her ventures. She introduced me to the CEO of her commercial investment company, whose mission deeply resonated with me, as it aimed to democratize access to investments typically reserved for the affluent while fostering a culture of confidence, innovation, and philanthropy. This encounter ignited a passion, leading me to facilitate connections between investors and commercial opportunities, ultimately flourishing into a rewarding role as an acquisition consultant. I've immersed myself in various investment groups, reveling in networking, event hosting, and all facets of real estate investing, particularly multifamily developments. As I delve deeper, my drive to empower women in this domain intensifies, recognizing their indispensable influence in shaping future generations.

"If you don't like the road you're walking, start paving another one." — Dolly Parton

"If one advances confidently in the direction of their dreams, and endeavors to live the life which they have imagined, they will meet with success unexpected in common hours." —Henry David Thoreau

We all navigate through life's transitions, challenges, and opportunities, continuously re-creating our empires with each hurdle we overcome. In my 50s, I faced a daunting divorce without a career to lean on; I stepped into the unknown. If I could muster the courage to start anew, so can you. Seek your dreams, passions, and ways to serve others, paving a path to prosperity. When it feels like everything is crumbling, remember, it might just be falling into place. I trust in a guiding force, but regardless of your beliefs, keep striving for your goals; they are within your grasp. Growth, learning, and experience shape us, molding our character. Surround yourself with a supportive network, and if you lack one, reach out and connect. Let's foster a community where we uplift each other, share successes, and help every woman create her empire. Let's shine together, each wearing our crowns proudly, as we navigate the journey ahead.

CHAPTER THREE

Jennifer Wright

Inspired Phoenix Enterprises

Creative Home Solutions

Owner

www.creativehomesolution.net
www.loansdonewright.org
https://www.linkedin.com/in/jennifer-wright-realestateinvesting/
https://www.instagram.com/jennifer_wright_rei/
https://www.tiktok.com/@jenniferwright1969
https://www.facebook.com/scorpiojenn/

Jennifer Wright epitomizes a unique fusion of empathetic leadership, entrepreneurial flair, and steadfast devotion to community welfare. Her extensive array of experiences both in her career and personal life positions her as a guiding light, offering support and motivation to many. With a rich background in Health Care Administration, Jennifer has augmented her professional credentials by obtaining certifications as a Board Certified Clinical Chaplain (BCC), Senior Transition Specialist (STS), and Certified Life Coach, showcasing her holistic dedication to assisting those in need.

In her capacity as a Bereavement Coordinator and Senior Transition Specialist, Jennifer demonstrates a profound understanding of the intricate facets of grief, loss, and life changes, extending a compassionate hand to individuals traversing these challenging paths. Her leadership acumen is evident through her roles as President of Valley West Rotary and Chairman of the Planning Commission, where she has spearheaded community development projects and encouraged civic participation, fostering tangible enhancements within her community.

Jennifer's commitment to advocacy and support is further evidenced through her tenure as Chairman of the Brain Injury Coalition, advocating for resources and awareness to improve the lives of those affected by brain injuries. As a Non-Profit Board Member and Life Coach, she leverages her strategic foresight and empathetic demeanor to empower both individuals and organizations, fostering personal and professional growth while strengthening community ties.

As an International Speaker, Jennifer shares her expertise on diverse subjects such as business success, real estate investment, healthcare administration, and humanitarian efforts, captivating audiences worldwide with her engaging presentations. In the realm of real estate and mortgage lending, she is revered as a trusted advisor and astute investor, exemplified by her company, Inspired Phoenix Enterprises, dedicated to providing ethical and solution-oriented services to homeowners facing challenges.

Central to Jennifer's multifaceted endeavors is her role as a Mother and Grandmother, which instills in her a profound appreciation for family values and community cohesion. Her dedication to her loved ones serves as a driving force behind her professional pursuits, anchoring her in principles of love, integrity, and service.

Jennifer Wright's life journey embodies a tapestry of compassionate leadership, entrepreneurial drive, and unwavering commitment to enriching the lives of others. Through her roles as a businesswoman, healthcare advocate, community leader, and family cornerstone, Jennifer continues to inspire and uplift those around her, epitomizing purpose-driven success.

Like a Phoenix Rising

by Jennifer Wright

"It's time to pack up your sleeping bag, sweetheart so that we can go to Mommie's college class," I say to my 2-year-old daughter inside our 2-person purple tent. We have been living in it up in the mountains by Snowbasin ski resort over the spring and summer months. Why were we living in a tent? Because we were homeless.

I was going to college and working in cardiology at a hospital. I couldn't afford daycare and wasn't getting any money from my daughter's father, as he left us when he found out I was pregnant after we had been dating for almost a year. He said he strongly desired to see other women and didn't want to be a father. So, my sweet little miracle daughter Ariel and I were alone.

Why was Ariel my miracle baby? At age 17, I had to have a tumor the size of a grapefruit removed from my right ovary and part of my left ovary removed as well. I told them they were not going to take my left ovary because I was going to be a mother one day. I felt this inside my soul. The surgeon said it was not safe and that my health was at risk. I told them again not to take both my ovaries—I would be fine and am going to have children. My parents told the surgeon that if I felt that way, I was probably right because I have a way of knowing things like this. After surgery, I woke up, and they were able to save part of my left ovary. So, having Ariel was not a mistake; she was a miracle and a gift from God. She was also born 6 weeks early through an emergency c-section, cord wrapped around her neck, footlong breach, placenta abruption, and placenta previa weighing 4 pounds.

CREATING HER EMPIRE

Growing up, I was raised LDS, Mormon. I was the eldest of a large family. Church and work were the most important thing, it seemed, to my parents. Being of service in their church callings was paramount. Raising good, Christlike children was crucial to our upbringing. We were sheltered when I was young. I always questioned our religion and wondered why things were the way they were and why this and why that. Something inside of me always felt there was something more. I questioned everything. If we were created in God's image, there must be a heavenly mother. And if they were our parents, they wouldn't love or accept their children just because they didn't believe or follow everything they did. So why should I feel less than or bad, sick, and wrong for having a beautiful baby?

In college, I was part of the LDSSA—the leadership team for the LDS Institute. I was also on the ballroom and dance team. I had been very spiritual my entire life. I just was not religious. I read all the different religious texts, attended many religious churches, and had many friends from other religions. So, when I became a single parent and had my daughter out of wedlock, I had to talk with my bishop and stake president. I was told that because I did not have remorse or feel guilty for having a child out of marriage, I had a difficult decision to make. I told them I would remove my name from the church. I felt so betrayed and abandoned. I felt that my daughter was not a mistake. I was told I might not be able to have children. She was my miracle. I was more hurt that I felt so alone and abandoned by my faith and some of my family, more than I was that my daughter's father left us. But at the same time, I felt such peace that I started my journey to find my path and purpose. Now that I'm older and wiser, I know that if I had told my dad and other members of my extended family how much I was struggling, they would have helped me. Lesson learned.

I was no longer welcome at my mother's, and my father lived in Texas. They got divorced when Ariel was 6 months old. My grandparents told me I made my bed, so I got to lay in it." Which meant I got pregnant outside of marriage, and so I had to live with the consequences. I was staying with my mother when I came back from Texas for about a month when Ariel was 1. My mother found out I drank a wine cooler and broke her rule of not obeying the word of wisdom, so she told me Ariel, and I would have to move out. We had no place to go.

I was the eldest of a large family and had an adventurous spirit. Growing up, I was very self-sufficient and had worked since I was 12 on our ranch as a nanny and candy striper. I have always wanted to be in healthcare, and my parents said I was born with a stethoscope. I've always had a nurturing soul and a gypsy spirit. I guess that led me to travel worldwide and work in healthcare, as a firefighter, and as a Humanitarian. I was driven and successful at anything I put my mind to. I had experienced sexual and physical trauma, grief, and loss many times growing up and kept that to myself. Being in a strong LDS family, there are some things you just don't talk about. So when I was experiencing struggle on my own with Ariel, and asking for help and then not getting it, I learned that I had to do things on my own because if I couldn't even rely on family or my faith, then Ariel and I were my family and I sought spirituality and support in other places.

I worked 12-hour shifts and went to college full-time. Ariel would go to daycare when I was at work but went to all my college classes because I couldn't afford daycare for school and work. I couldn't afford groceries, so we lived on top ramen, bread, peanut butter, and honey. I was making minimum wage, and everything I made went to daycare, gas in my car, diapers, and food for my daughter. I worked as much as possible to get overtime to pay for food and save money to get an apartment or rent a room with other college students and not live in the tent, as fall and winter would be coming, and it was already getting cold. I wasn't on Medicaid and took care of her myself.

I felt abandoned and alone. Yet, I never felt lonely, as my daughter Ariel and I were best friends. My professors loved having her in class, as she would sit at her own desk with her coloring book, pens, etc., and just sit next to me and do her own "homework." She and I did everything together.

After the summer was over and the fall chill was upon us, I found an abandoned house in Kaysville with power still turned on. I went to a thrift store, bought an electric top to cook with, and found a mattress and a chair on the road. Ariel and I lived in the abandoned house's basement for six months. One of my work friends found out what my living situation was, got together with others, and raised money to put a deposit down on an apartment for me in Salt Lake, right by the state capital.

I was promoted at the hospital and moved to Salt Lake from Ogden. I was still going to school in Ogden, but I needed a change of scenery as there were too many negative memories and too much energy in Ogden. While working at LDS Hospital, I was promoted quickly and given leadership and managerial jobs at such a young age. Others saw my worth even though I didn't see it. I was asked to be a delegate for the election and was the youngest delegate in our area. This opportunity opened up many avenues for me as influential people saw my worth, dedication, drive, intelligence, and compassion.

Yet, I battled with my self-worth. How could I be lovable, worthy, or successful when I felt abandoned and unloved by Ariel's father, some of my family, and God? I vowed that I would not let this happen to anyone else. I vowed to learn about all the resources in the community for single parents, homelessness, and those less fortunate. I promised I would be a source of healing and love. I vowed to find opportunities to serve people experiencing homelessness and the less fortunate. I vowed to see the God of my understanding and find a spirituality that spoke to my soul.

These fantastic experiences empowered me and gave me a sense of purpose. I sought after people of influence in areas where I would make the most impact. By aligning myself with influential people, doors I had not expected opened for me. I was asked to serve on the planning commission and was nominated as Chairperson. I was voted in as the President of our local Rotary International. I was made the Diplomatic Liaison to the Turkish American Society, working with the British Consulate while I was in Turkey. I was made the Chairman of the Brain Injury Coalition. This was all before the age of 30. I continued that passion for being of service through Humanitarian efforts with SHEROES United, Global Life Vision, Child Trafficking Rescue, and the Red Cross.

Mindset, self-reflection, and searching for meaning through trials and tribulations gave me my inner voice that genuinely loves people and wants to empower others. Experiencing homelessness, the suicide of my children's father, losing my husband to cancer, being cheated on, watching my brother die from drug and alcohol addiction, recovering myself from a stroke after getting a blood clot from a Humanitarian mission at the Vatican where I fell in a manhole and fractured my pelvis, death of my unborn child, rape, and abuse and more created my purpose. My purpose is to create worldwide abundance, joy within, and passion by living my spiritual life with unconditional love, empowerment, patient teaching, and compassionate healing.

I rise like the Phoenix, to burn even brighter than before, and come to those who truly need me. All my years of experience in service have led me to have such passion and compassion. Spirituality, to me, is LOVE. That is my religion. That is why I became a Clinical Chaplain and life coach. That is why I became a Mortgage Broker and real estate investor. In these areas, I could do the most good. In these careers and callings, I could impact and create change and generational wealth for me and everyone. There is so much to be thankful for. Gratitude is the key to abundance. What we are grateful for and what we give our attention to expands.

CHAPTER FOUR

Tamra Wright

Wright Investment Network

Owner

http://www.tamrahamblin.com
https://www.facebook.com/tamrahamblin
https://linktr.ee/tamrawright

Tamra is a best-selling author and real estate investor. She teaches others how to safely invest, pay less in taxes, and build generational wealth. Tamra loves to help others succeed and achieve more than they believed originally possible through encouragement, direction, guidance, education, and support.

Tamra has lived her life with her heart on her sleeve, so she has earned a lot of scars and life training, which she shares with others openly. She is a firm believer in teamwork and "group think" when it comes to learning new strategies and skills to succeed in life. She feels best when helping others with something that will help them live a better, more fulfilling life.

Mrs. Wright is married to Mr. Wright, with 5 boys and 10 grandchildren. She loves animals and enjoys spending time with her Long-Haired Chihuahua lap dog and camping with her family.

What the Heck? Oh! I Get It Now!

By Tamra Wright

In 2007, I gave a presentation to a group of professionals explaining how to effectively use social media to find employment. At the end of the meeting, I was told repeatedly that I should be an entrepreneur. I remember thinking, "What the heck does that mean, is that a compliment or something bad? What would I even do?"

Fast forward a few years, and I wasn't doing well at all, physically or mentally. I couldn't remember how to get back home from the neighborhood grocery store. I forgot my kids' names, and at times, I forgot I even had kids! In the mornings, I would wake up and think... nothing. There was no memory of tasks I needed to complete, appointments, excitement for future events, or frustrations from arguments the night before; nothing. It was extremely hard to get out of bed because I had no inspiration, motivation, or aspirations. I was losing everything, and it was getting worse. There was nothing I could do to halt it, no way to slow it down, and no idea why it was happening. I was so scared! Well, when I remembered what was happening, I was scared, but I frequently forgot it was happening. For those people who wonder if people with dementia or Alzheimer's realize they're losing their memory, I can tell you yes, they do, but they often forget even that.

This lasted for a few years, and I only have a couple of memories of those years. One memory was of being at a doctor's appointment and feeling anxious because I had to tell the doctor something before I forgot it again, but then when I told her, she sighed loudly and said, "Yes, you already told me that. Twice." After that appointment, I was so afraid I would forget to tell someone key information but was even more afraid of repeating myself and irritating people. I was losing my battle with life, and I hated it!

I had an MBA, and I graduated Cum Laude before the memory problems started, but I couldn't function anymore. I couldn't remember words, how to structure a sentence, different forms of your and you're, or how to use apostrophes. I would frequently start a sentence, but by the time I got to the end of it, I forgot what I was trying to express. My sentences didn't make sense, and people quit talking to me unless they absolutely had to. I spent most of my time watching TV because I couldn't function or do anything effectively and didn't dare leave the house unless I absolutely had to.

We still don't know why I experienced memory loss; there were no medical causes we could find, but it gradually improved and resolved itself. I will never forget the feeling of not knowing where I was, even when I was in my own bedroom and waking up to a blank slate, though. It was very lonely and depressing. I would not recommend it!

After my memory improved, I started my adult life over. I bought into an education program that offered personal coaching and self-improvement opportunities, as well as real estate investing training. I spent the next few years working to improve myself and my life. I could have given up and ended it all, but through the grace of God, I didn't.

Eventually, I wanted to meet with other investors and learn about strategies other people were using in our local market, so I kept waiting for someone to organize meetings and got frustrated when I realized no one saw my vision that I hadn't told anyone about (isn't that weird?). I'm not sure how I expected someone to know what I wanted or even why I felt like someone else needed to organize meetings, but I didn't feel like I could manage it and didn't know how to organize an event. My loving and totally supportive husband, though, helped me, and we started offering meetings in our area.

Our first meeting was successful, and we had 50 people attend! We had great feedback and enjoyed seeing old partners and meeting new entrepreneurs. However, I was too afraid to get up in front of the group I created! I was a nervous wreck all night; I asked another investor to lead MY meeting. I sat in the front row, wishing I was brave enough to lead the group I pulled together and kicking myself for being so weak. It was heartbreaking.

We held meetings on a weekly basis for two months, and I didn't dare lead any of them, but eventually, we had to admit defeat. Very few people found the meetings as wonderful as we did and it just wasn't worth the effort, so we decided to quit holding them, but then the strangest thing happened. The same day we discussed closing, we were invited to lead another group! We had support from other investors, access to free marketing, and seven investors ready to join right away. Even though it wasn't in a location we wanted (it was an hour away), we said yes and created weekly events.

Our first meeting was a hit, and this time, the second meeting was too! Within a month, we had 10 people attending regularly. Within two months, there were 20. Each month, we attracted more people and the feedback continued to be positive, so we developed relationships with other groups to combine with and build each other up. If we hadn't started that first group, though, we never would have found our stride and been invited to lead the next group. We had to be willing to roll with the changes and do what we could to make things happen in our lives.

For years, I've heard things like, "If you want something different, you have to make the change," which makes sense, but I never knew how to do it literally. You can't just make up your mind to change and then do it. Right? You need to know what you want to change, have a vision of what you want your life to become, and have some goals to work towards. I knew I wanted my life to be different and wanted "more," but couldn't envision what that meant or what changes to make.

It was like wanting to go somewhere but not knowing the destination or how to get there.

I eventually discovered that I could make small changes, that each change would take me further from where I was, and that I could constantly evaluate and implement corrective actions as needed. Pretty soon, I was in a different place, doing different things with different people, and if I didn't like where I was, I could tweak it to get to where I wanted! Previously, I thought I had to take huge steps to change my life, but now I realize I don't need to make big changes, like moving across the country, to change my life. Just small things, like smiling at strangers, speaking up, asking questions I keep hoping someone else will ask, saying hello to someone different, etc., will eventually change my scenery, and I'll go from being alone to being surrounded by people who are full of life!

Sometimes, when you're faced with changes, you've just got to roll with it. Things don't always go as planned, but not all changes are bad. If you believe something, your subconscious will work to prove it or make it happen, so if you believe you're a failure, you will fail. If you fully believe you can succeed, you will find a way to make it happen. Even if everything is stacked against you and you cannot see how to succeed, keep going, trying, and improving. When it looks and feels so dark you can't see your hand in front of your face, when you feel alone and abandoned, don't quit. If you stop, you are guaranteed to fail. If you keep going, at least you have a chance of improving your circumstances and winning.

I've learned so much! Now, I help people see the value they bring to the table and their potential; I encourage them to keep going. My life is amazing, and I'm so glad I didn't give up even though I felt alone and didn't know where I was headed! Each week, I stand in front of the room and introduce our speaker. I'm making progress and overcoming the fear of being in front of an audience. It's taken me almost 20 years, but I'm starting to understand what being an entrepreneur means and finding my path; it's very exciting, and I get it now!

If I could give any tips, it would be these:

- Never quit or give up
- Be open to new experiences
- Take small steps to change what bothers you
- Breathe through the fear when it comes because it will come
- Look forward, don't live in the past
- Look for solutions, don't accept failure from yourself
- You are worthy and worth more
- You are only alone if you choose to be

Go get 'em!

CHAPTER FIVE

Michelle Torres

Titan

CEO

https://www.instagram.com/utrealtor.michelle/whttps://www.facebook.com/michelle.torres.520/

My name is Michelle Torres. I'm a wife & a mother to 7. I've been a realtor & investor for 21+ years, as well as a business owner to a local tire shop. I enjoy being a business woman and am very proud of all my accomplishments.

Courage & Kindness to Ourselves

◆

By Michelle Torres

Have you ever thought about how many women overcome the challenges and obstacles in their daily lives? What challenges did they have that were different from yours? Were there some that had the same ones?

I am sure many women may have had the same challenges, but not many have dared to push through those challenges. I feel that my first challenge began in high school, being a minority woman with many racial gestures toward me. Trying out cheerleading, gymnastics, and dance, I was always put to the side. I made the team but was always last in everything they offered. Even though I was put to the side many times, I told myself I needed to build courage If this was life. So, courage and kindness were for me, not them, which gave me the strength to stand up for what I believed in. Life began when I had my first child and lost her at 2 months old. It was devastating to me, and felt like my world was upside down. I had another child, and that relationship failed six months after having him. Seven years later, I had 3 more, and I felt like I was a failure bringing children into the world. Being a single mother, I felt exhausted and overwhelmed, not even having time for them or myself. When I meet my husband. I brought 4 children into the marriage. He took on the role of being a father to my children; oh, was I thankful that I was able to stay home and rear my children while he supported us. Time went on, and I had a car accident, then another one a few years later. That's when some of my challenges started. I was in pain, in surgery, juggling my children and taking care of the finances. Oh, let's not forget playing the role of a housewife. There were days when I felt lost, broken, and overwhelmed. the days would pass by, then the months, then the years. It felt like my time was going by so slowly. It felt like I could not even accomplish anything I wanted to do. It seemed like I had become a single, married mother doing it all. Not even being able to clock in and out to make a paycheck. Then again, another car accident, another surgery, I was on the clock 24/7. Constantly trying to recover from all that pain and misery. Time after time, I faced many challenges and obstacles. I had dreams and plans of who I wanted to be, so I started working toward them slowly As I was recovering and rearing my children. My husband decided he wanted to have children of his own. So before I met him, I had my tubes tied. I Said I do not have any more children. Well, it happened. I found a doctor in North Carolina. I called and made an appointment. and before you knew it, we were flying to North Carolina. I came home, and a week later, we went to Mexico. After a few days, I had a really bad infection from the surgery. That gave me a break from my daily chaos. I started taking classes for my real estate, and I found out that I was pregnant. I went to take my test for my licenses. It actually took me seven times. How frustrating it was, at the same time, finding out that We were going to have a baby. Well, two months later, I lost the baby to a miscarriage, got pregnant again about 4 months later, and had a girl. A year later, I got pregnant again and had another miscarriage. I ended up having another baby girl two years later. I was so stressed out, well, here I was again, starting all over having new babies; with that being said, I now have a total of 6 children, 4 of them being teenagers. What a handful! That alone was another challenge trying to juggle all of their needs. As well as starting a career. Wow, talking about challenges here, I am putting more on my plate; I learned how to build courage and deal with all of these obstacles over time. It's not an easy thing to do, but the willingness to act despite having the fear of not overcoming them. Where would I be? What may have happened? We can ask ourselves if courage is something you're born with or if it can be learned. I felt like I learned it over time because, at times, it was so overwhelming. How many women would have given up? I had dreams and plans of who I wanted to be, so I started working toward them slowly. I started by taking real estate classes to become a realtor/ Investor. I knew if this were the type of work and the career I would be doing, I would be able to work my schedule around my husband's, meaning that I would work when he was off. I was willing to take risks and act like I had everything figured out; I knew I could do it. I was tired of everyone telling me that I couldn't make it, that I was crazy to try and start a new business while rearing my children, especially having two small babies. Fast forward, it was maybe five years into doing real estate when I became sick, cysts growing in my stomach, and My doctor told me that I had to have surgery the next day and it was going to be a full hysterectomy. Oh, my world was devastated again, what my husband and children were going to have to deal with, me going through another surgery and being put into full menopause. It was going to be a nightmare, and it was. For months, I was not myself. My husband was like your doctor told me: remember that if you love your wife, she will not be herself. There are days that you won't even know her. She will be very emotional, and she will cry for no reason; she will fight and argue, and It will be hard. My husband never told me what the doctor said until months later; as days went by, I felt all these things that my doctor told my husband. He ended up telling me all the things that the doctor said when we got in.

There were some really bad fights. There were days that we were going to divorce; I remember going into the bathroom crying in the mirror and asking myself why are you like this. I started to cry and was mad at myself for these things. I knew that I needed self-help. I started seeing a doctor and a therapist for some time. This helped me build up some courage to continue on. Years had gone by, and I started getting a little bit better. I was thankful for my husband being somewhat understanding. So, I returned to doing my real estate and investing. My husband decided he no longer wanted to work at his job, where he had been working for over 18 years. He decided that he wanted a business. Yes, we opened up the tire shop in 2015. I put my real estate on hold again. To get the tire shop up and running, I was working in the office and doing real estate; in 2019, I was in another car accident That damaged my whole left side, Leaving me unable to walk, to a rotator cuff surgery that left me out for about 8 months to a year. This was my 2nd rotator cuff surgery. You know, I was looking for the courage I had in my younger days, telling myself you still have it. I know that being courageous can be incredibly rewarding. It can lead to personal growth, positive change, and a deeper sense of self-respect. I knew that I had to find it and fast. I knew that this was going to help heal me. I was on my road to recovery, working on myself and helping to run two businesses. It's been a struggle. I have two daughters helping in the office and one of my sons working in the shop. I am grateful for rentals that bring me cash flow.

My husband supported me through some of the challenges that I went through, and there were many challenges he did not help support me in, And Real estate was one of them.

On October 17, 2023, I was hit by a semi/diesel. Wow, another hit that re-triggered all of my 2019 symptoms; despite another accident and setbacks, I am working on my recovery. Another head concussion, I am still seeking help from different doctors. I believe that the many challenges I faced over the years have made me a strong woman. I Will not let anyone put me down; if these struggles cannot keep me down, nothing will. I am now in the process of getting my construction licenses, and I have opened up a new construction company.

Who is stopping you from getting what you want? Is it your self-talk? What are you telling yourself? We women struggle in life. Who pays us women to clock in and out taking care of our children? Who made sure we had social security benefits for us? This is why I kept building the courage to go on every day. I had to do it for myself.

All you need is courage and always be kind to yourself.

CHAPTER SIX

Shay Stone

PopRock Fitness and Nutrition/PopRock Realty

Owner, Certified Nutritionist and Personal Trainer/ Real Estate Agent and Developer

poprockfitness.com
https://www.tiktok.com/@poprockfitnesscoaching?_t=8luYBrNS0h4&_r=1
https://www.instagram.com/shaystone13/?igsh=MTJrOGJ0MDJiYncxOA%3D%3D

Shay Stone has built her Estate Empire in the Mountains of Utah. She has created three businesses as a single mother raising her two incredible boys. After her own hard life struggles, her journey of self-discovery has helped hundreds of people on their paths. She is a Certified Nutritionist, Personal Trainer, and Yoga Instructor and has worked for decades with athletes of all ages to help them rediscover themselves and reconnect with their bodies. In 2020, her expertise in finance shifted her path into the world of Real Estate. Her self-conquering attitude and ambition for life are contagious as she trains others on how to break their own physical boundaries. This same passion is what has helped her to transcend successfully through multiple business industries.

I would love to help anyone this may connect with my story. In food, health, or Real Estate. Reach out. Text, email, or call me, Let me help you, rediscover you.

Conquer Yourself

◆

by Shay Stone

What if I told you I could teach you how to eat, lose weight, gain muscle, build the body of your dreams, and I could do it all with healthy, easy, yummy, real food, would you?

Eating pizza, pasta, hamburgers, french fries, chocolate, crackers, and popcorn. You can have steak, sushi, and a night out. You don't have to cut out carbs, desserts, or any food group. You can let go of any guilt.

What if I could teach you how to eat in a pattern, for your body, in the right amounts, so you would never doubt what your body needed ever again?

I can. Truth.

I've helped people transition or transform their lives through the power of food and movement. I work with children, teens, athletes, women, and men of all ages, as well as the elderly.

Clients have shed hundreds of pounds, overcome eating disorders, become pregnant after infertility, faced their greatest fears, lost loved ones, and healed from past or present trauma.

Everyone has a story of self-discovery. This is mine…

I am a girl of the '90s/2000s. It was the era of the super thin supermodels, boy bands, and fad diets. At that time, a woman couldn't be thin enough, and muscles were only sexy on men.

My mother was always on a diet. She had her special diet food, her scale, and measuring cups, and she was always trying the next new thing.

I'm smack dab in the middle of 11 children. No twins, just crazy parents. A 1000-acre farm, 500 head of cattle, dozens of horses, pigs, goats, lamas, rabbits, and birds galore.

I slept in a 100-year-old attic room with my five sisters, sharing a bed with one for most of my life. We had one small bathroom, all 13 of us shared. During the summer, we slept outside, watching for SkinWalkers, and we'd catch salamanders in the flooded basement. Winters would get so cold our hair would break off as we ran barefoot to catch the school bus before dawn.

We were taught that life is work, and we were born to do so. We tilled, planted, watered, picked, canned, cleaned, and stored. We milked the cows and fed the babies. We were completely self-sufficient and utterly dirt-poor.

At 15, I had the body of a woman and wished for a young girls. I had curves — Double D's and an hourglass figure that many men would covet. I hated it. I would binge/purge and starve myself, hoping to be thin. My self-value is based on my body. My hypocritical mother would scream, I am destroying my body, all while she was betraying and damaging hers with Fen/Phen, Keto, Palio, HCG, Jenny Craig, Fasting, etc.

At 16, when the second Twin Towers went down, I was in my trauma medical class. I watched and wished I could help the victims. I had training and the disaster had shifted me, as it did many. My plans to join the military, for the college grants, and to become a helicopter nurse were halted by begging from my parents and a fear of real danger. Memories of Vietnam still live in their heads.

Instead, I graduated a year early with honors, college credits, and straight A's.

I was fascinated with anything related to the body—cells, bones, blood, muscles—and how it functions. I studied sports medicine, helping athletes with torn joints or bones protruding through their skin. I became an EMT, studied nursing, and started work at the hospital.

I had been away for close to a year. While my friends partied on what was supposed to be my graduation night, I stood on the streets of New York, looking up at the only thing left of The Twin Towers. Two beams — resembling a perfect cross. A symbol of human loss. Rubble from buildings still in the streets. The loss of life lingering in the air from months before. I knew I was meant to help people heal.

I fell in love. He was incredible, sweet, handsome, and kind. One day, he got incredibly sick. We had a silly fight that night over spoiled plans. I was upset. The next day, I couldn't find him. I called several times. - Nothing. I Stopped by. -Nothing. I went to work, anxious. I found him- in the ICU, unconscious and on life support. I didn't expect those delicate moments to be our last. I kissed his lips. My tears fell onto his pale skin. I silently plead for forgiveness, sending love through my fingertips. Why do goodbyes have to be so gut-wrenching? Leaving you debilitated, screaming, fighting, and searching for your soul. Nothing in this world is more valuable than time. Time is precious, and so are hugs and kisses; give them freely to those you love. Not everyone is blessed with the gift of growing old.

I couldn't keep walking into the same hospital where I was haunted by the ghosts in my memory, fighting to save someone's loved one, unable to save my own. I flew to Kenya and then Uganda, serving in the hospitals and orphanages. Seeing the plague of aids, the quantity of orphaned children, starvation, lack of clean water, unavailability of medical care, and mass deaths transformed my soul. I left my heart with the African people.

On the 4th of July, after a 36-hour delay because of a car bomb explosion being set off in the airport we were in, I watched fireworks explode over the Statue of Liberty as we dropped into New York. My gratitude for food, water, shoes, paper, and tampons would never be diminished.

I took a job at a bank. I worked in customer service, then ACH/Payment Processing, Accounts/loans, and asset recovery. In 2008, our bank went under and was taken over by the government, then sold off. It was one of the hardest times of my life. I was in charge of running all operations for two banks at one time, along with auditing each morning, noon, and night. Our staff was cut, as was our pay. I packed on the pounds from stress.

I felt off. Something was different. It happened one day while pregnant with my second son. I remember feeling a strange change in my body. "When you say a change... like... a personality shift?" My doctor had finally asked the right question. My eldest had just turned 2, and my second, just 3 months. A scan confirmed a tumor in the back of my brain.

I was 29. I had everything I could have ever wanted, and I was miserable. I had lost myself - In motherhood and wifehood. I was living the dream I was told would make me happy instead of listening to my own intuition. If I only had a short life left, I wanted to LIVE.

I wanted my children to believe in themselves. I needed to believe in myself. I needed to teach them how to battle their darkest days. I had to overcome it on my own. Your reaction to a situation is what builds your character. That happiness is a choice. I wanted to be happy.

I was overweight. My bones ached, and my joints cracked. I had high blood pressure and couldn't walk up a flight of stairs. To live, I needed to heal my body.

I started lifting weights - I FELL IN LOVE.

It gave me the strength to face my demons.

Like everything valuable in life, it took time, patience, and work.

After 13 years, I left my stable, high-paying job in pursuit of happiness and purpose. I became a Trainer/Coach. I found balance and spirituality with Yoga and became an instructor. I learned what it meant to fuel the body as an athlete. That 80% is what you put in your body and 20% your workouts. I learned what carbohydrates, protein, and fats do and how to balance macronutrients. I hired a coach and trained my body, this time, with food. I wanted to conquer myself - My weight, genetics, mental and emotional health, and my demons.

Commitment and consistency are key. Each day, I stayed committed to myself. I built the woman I wanted to become. Belief in myself was the first step in building my Empire. Healing myself from the inside out. My skin cleared up and started glowing. My stomach flattened. My gut biome changed, and period cramps disappeared. I didn't need caffeine. My body was getting stronger. Muscles popped. I never got sick. — All because I was fueling my body with real food in a balanced diet of 40% carbs, 40% protein, and 20% fats. I was eating 4 fruits and 5 cups of veggies daily. I ate whole foods, limited my fats, and drank 100 oz of water each day. I lifted heavy 5 days a week and ate enough protein. Consistency and mental focus shifted to all areas of my life. Long-forgotten traumas surfaced as my body was able to release, no longer focused on the poison from preservatives and sugar. Food fueled correctly was MAGIC. The key to all health.

I opened PopRock Fitness and Nutrition in 2016. I have coached hundreds of people on their health journeys over the last decade. I opened PopRock Teens/Kids in 2017, helping children disconnect from online and reconnect with their bodies. I devote the rest of my time to nutrition/health clients, my children, and as a Real Estate Agent and Investor.

Movement is life. In the gut, the muscle, home, or the soul. Growth doesn't come without discomfort. Pushing boundaries is my gift. Let me teach you how to Conquer yourself.

CHAPTER SEVEN

Emily South

Truevoice, LLC

Transformational Coach

https://www.findyourtruevoice.com
https://www.facebook.com/emiisouth/
https://www.instagram.com/emiique/
https://linktr.ee/findyourtruevoice

Emily South is a queer transformational coach and speaker passionate about empowering others to live their truest, most authentic, brave, and expansive lives. With 20 years of experience as an entrepreneur, digital marketing consultant, corporate trainer, and leadership coaching she helps clients achieve breakthroughs at the crossroads of personal and professional life. Emily South is a sought-after speaker who has inspired audiences worldwide to be mindful, authentic, and wholehearted in relationships, the spaces we embody, and life.

Emily takes an integrated holistic approach to coaching. She blends both western and eastern spiritual practices to support her clients' goals to let go of fears, release limiting beliefs, and take inspired action for ultimate well-being.

As a coach, Emily, thinks outside the box and firmly believes "Embracing diversity creates possibilities" for all humanity. Together we rise!

Free to BE all of me!

By Emily South

You will have the most important relationship with yourself. The journey of self-discovery is lifelong and often a revolution, an awakening, and a reclaiming of power. At the heart of this revolution lies the fundamental birthright – and the immense challenge – to speak our truth and live authentically. The way forward as a human race is to integrate, not segregate, all our parts. Life is a series of opportunities to explore what that means and grow and rise to our highest potential. As women, the invitation to color outside the lines and embrace all of you is knocking. Will you wake up and answer the call?

Living authentic is a choice and infinitely rewarding if you commit to it. Where there is more risk, there is more reward. Everything you are looking for is outside your comfort zone. Living brave and authentic means taking risks, staying open, and thinking outside the box of the present moment, expanding consciousness to love all your parts (mental, emotional, physical, energetically) as a multi-dimensional, multi-passionate being. It means you intentionally create space to bring all of you every day. It means boycotting the constructs and systems created to control and monetize our time and energy. It is your sovereign right to co-create with the universe and live independently of the limiting beliefs and imaginations of others.

Ready to make some noise and truly live your best life NOW and claim what is already yours? Ready to create space for new adventures, possibilities, and stories to unfold. Good, let's begin. We attract what we think, feel, and imagine! In other words, what we focus on enlarges. Change your thoughts and beliefs, and change your life. It's that easy!

The universe and life respond to what we truly desire. We are like magnets and attract who we are BEing. This is true for everything in life. We are literally creating our reality every day. Where are you putting your energy?

When you know better, you can do better and BE better. Life is a journey of discovery or unfolding. Stay curious and ask questions. It requires time and energy to be mindful of the conditioned mind and bold enough to let go of old beliefs and thought patterns that hold us back and adopt new, empowering ones. For example, when I came out as a transgender woman at age 39, I started asking deeper questions like "When will I feel happy in my body?" "Why am I drawn to the feminine?" "Who am I?" "Why am I here?" "What is my purpose?" "Who do I want to become?" and "What is truly important and why?" These questions unlocked a reservoir of courage to find a therapist to get to the root cause of my depression and suicidal thoughts. After multiple sessions, I was diagnosed with "gender dysphoria." This introduced me to the LGBTQIA+ community and a whole new world of possibility. I gave myself permission to piece together the puzzle of my life.

With the divorce, I left a toxic marriage of 11.5 years and a religious cult. Many nights, I cried myself to sleep, missing my four beautiful children, two girls and two boys. Then it dawned on me. Everything in life is a choice – thoughts, words, feelings, and beliefs. I chose to live and gave myself permission to embrace my feminine side and create a new reality.

My choice to seek answers and a therapist led me to the truth that set me free from a prison of my own making. I took the road less traveled, stopped conforming, and trusted my intuitive rebel heart.

There was a powerful message in the mess of coming out. When we create space to love all our parts, follow our hearts, and live authentically, it's like a huge weight is lifted off our shoulders, allowing us to be present, open, feel safe, and quiet the inner soul. As I connected with life, abundance, and unconditional love, the light grew, and so did my confidence, to eclipse and transform all the pain and uncertainty into peace, power, wisdom, and purpose.

Asking questions and becoming mindful of the answers gives us a peek into how our subconscious drives our lives. Most importantly, it means we can integrate all our parts to work in harmony from the inside out.

Let's explore your truth or self-concept:

Understanding Your Truth

- Inner Compass: Your truth isn't a singular statement but a constellation of experiences, values, and beliefs that guide you. Start by identifying your core values. What matters most to you? Is diversity, equity, inclusion, justice, creativity, compassion, or intellectual growth? These values become your internal compass, guiding your decisions and actions.
- Owning Your Story: Our experiences shape who we are. Explore your past – the joys, the heartbreaks, the triumphs, and the failures. Examining these moments helps you understand your strengths, vulnerabilities, and the stories you tell yourself. Are these stories empowering or limiting? Reframing your narrative(s) allows you to let go of limiting beliefs, live in the present moment, and rewrite your future. Seek to know your own story; in the process, you will discover peace, power, and purpose.
- Embracing Your Voice: Your truth has a unique voice. It's not about imitating others but finding your own rhythm and tone. Pay attention to what ignites a spark within you. What topics make you want to speak up? What injustices move you to action? These passions are the embers of your authentic voice waiting to be fanned into a flame.

The path to authenticity is rarely a straight line. We often build walls around ourselves constructed from fear, societal conditioning, limiting beliefs, and the need for approval. So many people are afraid of rejection. But, ironically, when we don't honor our authentic voice or true feelings, we reject ourselves. Let's explore some obstacles.

Overcoming Obstacles

- **Fear of Rejection**: The fear of disapproval is a powerful silencer. We might worry about being judged, ridiculed, or ostracized. Remember, speaking your truth isn't about pleasing everyone. It's about living with integrity and attracting those who resonate with your authenticity.
- **People-Pleasing:** The constant need to please others can drown out our own voice. We prioritize validation over truth, sacrificing authenticity for acceptance.
- **Internalized Messages:** Throughout our lives, we've absorbed messages about who we "should" be. These messages can become internalized narratives, holding us from embracing our true selves.
- **The Need to Belong**: Humans are social creatures with a deep desire for connection. This can lead to a tendency to blend in and avoid rocking the boat. However, true connection thrives on authenticity. When you express your true self, you attract people who value and appreciate you for who you are.
- **The Inner Critic**: That nagging voice in your head, telling you you're not good enough, smart enough, or brave enough? That's your inner critic. Challenge its negativity. Practice self-compassion. Everyone makes mistakes, and vulnerability is a strength, not a weakness.

The first step to reclaiming your voice is acknowledging these barriers. Once identified, you can begin chipping away at them, employing these tools for self-discovery:

- **Self-awareness:** Practice introspection. Journal, meditate, or spend time in nature—activities that allow you to tune into your inner voice. Ask yourself: What brings me joy? What energizes me? What angers or frustrates me?
- **Values Clarification:** What core principles guide your life? Identifying your values helps you understand your "whys" and provides a compass for authentic expression.

Sorry, not sorry. It takes tremendous fortitude to carry on when you can see what others cannot. And to find light within the shadows. As we become more congruent and authentic living, both the light and the dark become our greatest teachers, and our capacity to live in the NOW increases. Everything in life becomes an opportunity to revisit/revise our internal narratives and tune in to higher vibrations by deciding what and who we want in life. With self-awareness as your foundation, you can now begin to build your empire of authenticity. Here are some strategies to express your truth with confidence:

- **Start Small:** Don't overwhelm yourself. Begin by speaking your truth in low-stakes situations. Share your honest opinion with a friend, and politely decline an invitation that doesn't align with your values. These small acts of self-expression build confidence and momentum.
- **Practice Assertiveness:** Develop the skill of assertively communicating your needs and desires. Assertiveness allows you to express yourself respectfully without being aggressive or passive.
- **Find Your Tribe:** Surround yourself with people who value authenticity and celebrate your unique voice. Seek mentors, communities, or online forums that resonate with your values.
- **Embrace Vulnerability:** Don't wait until you feel perfectly ready. Sharing your true self, vulnerabilities, and all, fosters deeper connections and genuine relationships. Vulnerability is not weakness; it's a sign of strength and courage.

Living Your Truth, Building Your Empire

Living authentic is a lifelong journey. There will be times when it feels easy and times when it requires immense courage. Remember, authenticity is the bedrock of a fulfilling life. When you live your truth, you inspire others to do the same. It's from this collective courage that empires are built, not just empires of wealth and power but empires of self-acceptance, connection, and positive change.

Embrace the M.A.G.I.C. that only you can bring into the world.

M – Mindfulness. Be where your feet are. It takes daily practice but gets easier. Be the observer in the space between stimulus and response. Next time a situation presents itself, take a deep breath, count to three, observe what thoughts and feelings arise, and then consciously choose a new empowering response. This helps you recognize when and how you hide authenticity.

A - Authentic. Create space to BE (breathe and expand) every day. Take the road less traveled by living authentically and remembering everything in life is a choice – thoughts, words, feelings, and beliefs. You can have and be anything you desire if you are willing to shift internally to manifest it. We create our realities from the inside out. Who will you become, and what will you do?

G – Gratitude. Practice gratitude daily. Expressing gratitude is associated with a host of mental and physical benefits. Mayo Clinic's health studies show that feeling thankful can improve sleep, mood, and immunity. Gratitude can decrease depression and anxiety. Buy a gratitude journal and write 5 things you are grateful for every day. It's a great way to get clear on who you are and what you desire to attract/create in life.

I – Intuition and Inspired Action. Begin with the end in mind. What can you do today, this week, and this month to get you closer to your goals? This is the final step of manifesting what you desire in life. We attract abundance, love, and serendipitous opportunities by trusting our intuition and taking inspired actions, leaving the details of the how and the when to the universe. When we create from an authentic space, we find ourselves in "the flow," receiving all that is lined up for us with gratitude, and the universe orchestrates everything for our highest good.

C—Stay curious. Embrace it all! Acknowledge and love all your parts as a multidimensional and multi-passionate human being. As we transcend our own limitations, our presence becomes a catalyst for the liberation of others. This interconnected dance expands our capacity to change the world from the inside out.

The journey to authenticity is an ongoing process. There will be moments of doubt and setbacks. However, each time you choose to speak your truth, your voice grows stronger, your confidence builds, and your empire expands. Remember, authenticity is not a destination; it's a continuous journey of self-discovery and empowered expression. Be the change you seek and live authentically in the NOW.

CHAPTER EIGHT

Amandha Zhane

Love is Freedom is Love

Evolutionary Explorer

https://www.youtube.com/@azhaneofficial
www.instagram.com/azhaneofficial

Amandha Zhane is an American TV host, lifestyle journalist, spiritual teacher, and artist. As a child, Amandha loved creating art and talking to animals. Amandha became a public figure in Utah as a TV host and feature reporter for the CBS and FOX affiliates in Salt Lake City. After certifying as a yoga teacher and becoming trained to teach meditation by Deepak Chopra, MD, Amandha founded The Dharana Method® of meditation in 2017. In 2020, she stepped away from the school at its peak after being fired from FOX during the pandemic - in the middle of a divorce. Social media broadcast her journey of moving into a travel trailer as a newly unemployed, single mom, where she learned from Native American teachers and got back in tune with herself and the Earth. Amandha lives in Sedona with her horse and leads retreats and creates art between visits from her favorite person in the Universe, her son, William.

Purpose is In Your Presence

◆

By Amandha Zhane

Woman, I feel your heart's longing.

I feel your desire to be heard, seen, and held in the experience of all that you deeply feel.

You long to feel safe to express yourself and have your needs met so that you can be free to nurture, create, and inspire.

What if your purpose was simply to live true to your nature? What if your true nature was something already there in you and has been since birth?

Perhaps you know this deep in your heart: That just *being you* is enough?

Even more than that, perhaps you see that just being you is the key to sustainable fulfillment.

Remember the simple joys of childhood? Remember the wonder of a new experience, even one so slight as a new taste or texture?

It wasn't until people started asking us what we wanted to be when we grew up that we learned to identify with a false world outside of the present moment. Before then, the present moment was good enough, and *we* were good enough, just as we were.

Perhaps you might practice cutting away all of the labels, identities, and expectations from the outside world (and the ones you have piled on yourself) until only the truth remains: Your love radiating, with the innocence of a child, in the ever-present now. We practice this in The Dharana Method® meditation.

I know, Woman, to be authentically you and present is difficult, especially as a mother, where you have many responsibilities, people to care for, and a million chances to skip self-care. I will agree with you when you tell me that you would LOVE to be present and child-like with your children, but that the world has demands and expectations of you to be something other than a mother! Or perhaps you are a single mother and do not have the resources and protection to be fully present with your children, even if you are connected to your present, purest Self. And even if you are not a mother or woman, you may find yourself without the resources and support of a partner so that you may live true to your nature of breathing with your emotions as you process the world within you and around you.

The world's wisdom traditions say that feminine energy is lunar in nature, and the internal world is our kingdom, where infinite possibilities are waiting to be birthed. Conversely, traditional wisdom says masculine energy is solar energy, meant to penetrate the feminine void with the light of its intention. Theirs is the kingdom of the external: Building, leading, conquering, destroying, protecting, defending, cultivating, refining, and harvesting.

According the Hinduism, the masculine Shiva danced with feminine Shakti and together, they birthed creation.

Based on these descriptions, does our current society allow masculine or feminine energies to be true to their nature?

Imagine how supported the Feminine would feel if the Masculine protected her and provided a safe place for her to feel, imagine, create, nurture, and transmute energy? Imagine how supported the Masculine would feel if he created this for her and received the support, nurturing, and Oracle guidance that the Feminine naturally provides when she can nurture herself.

During my divorce proceedings, the mediator made child support calculations based on me going back to work full-time and making a salary comparable to what I made full-time - before having my child. We now know that a mother's career can take ten years to recover from children. *[1]Research shows 44% of mothers earn less than what they made prior to having children. The same research states that the rising percentage of women forced into lower-paying jobs, coupled with the rising cost of childcare and layered with a lack of flexibility at the office, can create a lose-lose situation for mothers faced with going back to work.

At the time of my divorce, I worked part-time to nurture our 6-year-old son and contribute to the family resources. But adding a mortgage, plus car insurance and splitting healthcare costs, in addition to providing all the needs for a household, was not something I could do on my part-time salary. So I was devastated to hear that our society would rather send the mother away from her child than encourage the father to continue to provide at least a home for the mother of his child so she could continue nurturing him in the way he deserved until maturity.

I don't believe putting the burden of two households on the father is right, either. Even though fathers face considerably fewer career setbacks after children, including after divorce, it would serve the child for society to assist fathers (or the Masculine parent) in providing at least a home for the mother (or Feminine) parent.

I have spent the past four years resisting society's expectation for me to give up my right to nurture my son to maturity. This, even after losing my part-time job in the middle of a divorce. I moved into a camper trailer to relieve the pressure of maintaining a mortgage or skyrocketing

---

1 Source: https://www.careersafterbabies.org/careers-after-babies-report

rent. I also found flexible, meaningful work in a neighboring state and got equipped with the land and know-how to start a sustainable lifestyle, but my son's father could not come to terms with me - the nurturing parent for the past six years - bringing my son along with me, and seeing him on the weekends. So, I continue to find and build income streams that don't require me to put my son in daycare.

My experience trying to make ends meet while being there for my son falls in line with data from an Australian survey that says 32% of divorced mothers live below the poverty line.

* [2]"Data from the Household, Income, and Labour Dynamics in Australia (HILDA) Survey from 2001 to 2019 show that 32% of single women who have had at least one child and one previous de facto or legal marriage live below the poverty line. This is compared to 10% of women who have had at least one child and who are currently living in their still intact first marriage."

Not all women want to be in their Feminine as a nurturer. Some women are more comfortable with masculine energy, and some men are more comfortable with feminine energy. Both Masculine and Feminine energies deserve to be free to live true to their nature. However, considering the needs of children in particular, they deserve a society where a parent is supported in nurturing them to maturity without experiencing poverty.

If we want a society where women in their Feminine are free to honor their nature as Women and Mothers, as well as being allowed to be in tune with our body's cycles, the rhythms of the earth, and the energies we are feeling and processing moment to moment, we must resist the impossible expectations placed on us and insist on a new paradigm. The Masculine will naturally benefit from this new paradigm, as they will be supported in living out their purpose-driven missions.

---

2 Source: https://melbourneinstitute.unimelb.edu.au/__data/assets/pdf_file/0011/4134467/Breaking-Down-Barriers-Report-5-June-2022.pdf

Perhaps, dear Woman, you can start by coming back to the present moment and learning what you actually are, versus who you've been expected to be. Perhaps in the cutting away of what you are not, you will start to hear your heart's whisper. And perhaps your heart's whisper will tell you exactly what it wants. And just maybe - considering the law of attraction - following your joy leads to sustainable fulfillment, as you attract all that is meant for you. This approach requires that you live life as the being of love that you are, relinquishing the need to validate your existence with external accomplishments, as Dr. Gabor Mate once said. Simply living this way is the biggest act of resistance to how things are now, and others will be inspired to do the same. This will create a ripple effect in a society where, once again, it is safe to simply BE: A woman, a man, a child, an animal, and the Earth herself.

May you consider the idea that your purpose is remembering who you are, and you are free to believe that your purpose is as simple as following your heart's desires for the good of all, with harm to none.

Because, Woman, you deserve it. As the very Tree of Life, what is good for you is good for all.

CHAPTER NINE

Katie Jo Finai

Sage Canvas LLC

CEO

https://sagecanvas.com
Sage Canvas
www.linkedin.com/in/katie-finai-004318194
https://www.instagram.com/sagecanvas.ut/?hl=en
https://www.tiktok.com/@katiejosage

Katie Jo is a published author, artist, photographer, and international public speaker with a passion for world travel, humanitarian work, and preserving the wisdom of the ancients. She is a business owner of Sage Canvas, a wellness studio based in Lehi, Utah, a central hub for a variety of experts, teachers, and practitioners in energy healing modalities. Katie Jo is also a Reiki Master Teacher and Sound Healing Master Trainer and offers a comprehensive Shamanic Philosophy and Ceremonies course. She is a student of life with a deep passion for the story of humanity and the possibility of oneness and peace, a mother of five and in love with the rascally Polynesian who married her.

Trust, Luck, and Elbow Grease

◆

By Katie Jo Finai

"To thine own self be true" Shakespeare; Hamlet.

I stood outside the brick building on Main Street in Lehi, Utah. Light summer rain was falling. The smell of fresh moisture on the warm sidewalk floated into my nostrils. Cars buzzed by, creating whooshing background noise as they passed. The East side of the brick building was covered from foot to roof in thick ivy. If I reached my hand into it- perhaps another world would open. Perhaps a monster would grasp my fingers and pull me in.

I looked down at my suede ankle boots, toes touching the line between cobblestone and cement on the walkway. It may as well have been the edge of a cliff. My skinny jeans and linen blouse were growing leopard spots from the light misting. In the 100-year-old storefront window, a piece of plain paper advertised "SHOP FOR RENT" in thick black Sharpie.

Earlier that morning, I quit my job after a decade-long career that I thought would be my retirement. I never planned on leaving, and my heart felt broken and lost. With the 2020 pandemic, which shut down all social interaction, I had a brand-new baby, and my plans for childcare and returning to work were obliterated. I had tried to make the best of it- but babysitting options were gone, and the shimmering rainbow I planned to follow toward the golden treasure of my retirement had disappeared with them. My situation wasn't personal. Across the world women and mothers were affected dramatically. In the mass exodus, women left the workforce to care for their kids. But it felt personal.

I found myself wandering aimlessly along my small city street with a troubled heart and mind, unsure of where my income was going to come from- but knowing that I had a new baby who needed his mother, but also my teens from a first marriage who depended upon me financially.

I dialed the number written on the shop sign with my hands trembling. The next day, I was writing a check for the deposit to open my own studio.

Terrified but trusting.

I had no idea what was in store for me, with no financial backer or investors and a social lockdown, but I trusted that this was the next step for me. I trusted that the past decade of managing a high-end sales and retail business was enough of a foundation for me to launch a business of my own. I trusted that I could learn along the way and would be okay if I failed. I had found myself in similar situations before.

I've often heard, "Luck is when preparation meets opportunity." I also recognize in my own life that what seems like "luck" often feels a lot more like being backed into a corner. What looks like "preparation" (and is) is surviving until the next day.

What looks like "confidence" is the humility to change.

In life, we find ourselves repeatedly facing the dilemma of trusting and moving forward. Many times, these choices are the points of reference that change everything. We are at the precipice of risk with no guarantees about the outcome, and all we can do is trust, hoping that the preparation life has offered us has been enough.

"I'm so happy you get to follow your dreams!" I'm told weekly. "You're doing what I always wanted to do!" sometimes said with a twinge of jealousy. "You're so lucky!" I hear over and over.

As a polite and seasoned businesswoman, I respond with a smile and "Thank you." Flitting away with the small talk of public relations, I reflect upon the perceptions of others about me. I'm naturally introverted. I prefer to be alone in my house, with good coffee and music in the background, hours swirling by as I paint, write, or read. I find it luxurious if days can go by without me seeing or talking to anyone. My soul is bandaged and healed.

What I am known for is being a public speaker, saleswoman, and business owner.

My core strength is doing whatever it takes (with integrity) to provide for my kids and to get out of tough situations.

When I catalog my life history, the file titled "things you thought would work out but didn't" may be the largest. As I write about building an empire or knowing a woman's purpose, I can't help but see these files swirl through my memories like a Rolodex. Wouldn't it be nice if we all knew the destiny star we wanted to aim our arrow at and even nicer if we hit it? For me, most of my shots have been shots in the dark. My guiding stars offer glimmers of hope in the darkness more than the goals I've accomplished. The arrows I've aimed- tend to fly wild.

When I was seventeen, my first "sales job" was waiting tables at a trucker diner buffet. Retrospectively, this job taught me to "read the energy" within thirty seconds of greeting people. To finesse the intuitive service of delivering what customers need before they ask. When the kitchen was running behind, and I had no control over late meals, I learned how to assuage disgruntled people. I navigated the fine line of self-respect. I was happy to serve but not willing to cower to diners who were demeaning to me (or sexist) because of my position. I couldn't possibly know I was being prepared with skills that would transfer to a future career.

Life trekked on. I married, stayed at home with my young family, and did "side jobs" to support my husband's career and earn "extra" money. When the marriage ended, I found myself, like many women do, with no job history or education to list on paper and three young mouths to feed. I learned in the most excruciating way that everyone should prepare a way to provide for themselves whether they have a partner or not- because you never know if you will need to.

For the next decade, I worked three jobs. Two of them were freelance and flexible and the other was in sales- the only position I could find as a fresh divorcee whose employment background was limited. I worked on commission, learning through "trial by fire," studying, and practicing the art of sales. This quiet and introverted bookworm became the top sales leader in the company. I was responsible for over fifty percent of the overall annual sales as the business tripled gross profits under my management. When people tell me I'm so "lucky," I remember this time. The sales training CDs playing in the car on my commute to and from work, the seven days a week I worked for years in a row, missing Christmas Eve, weekends, and holidays, doing whatever it took to refine the edges of my business skills to provide for my children. My motivation and strength came from wanting to do my best for them and to keep a roof over our heads.

Joan of Arc was content to stay in the garden, but there were greater plans for her.

Through all of this, the only way I could keep the soul exhaustion at bay was to find solace and purpose in service. Once a month, I volunteered at cancer events. These experiences are some of my favorite memories. I was able to shift into a mindset of gratitude and compassion. It took my mind off my own troubles and trudging. I studied energy healing modalities, painted leather drums, became a Reiki Master Teacher, trained in Shamanism, and eventually facilitated drum circles as a way to create community and help lift hearts.

One early autumn day, I received a phone call from a friend as I was driving down the freeway in my ten-year-old SUV, "Katie, do you ever check your email?" she asked. "No. Not unless it's my work email." I responded. "Do you know you are the keynote speaker at the World Parliament of Religions?" she asked. My stomach dropped. I almost swerved into another road lane. "What?"

I had sent in an application months before to "volunteer" at this global event. I included a snippet of my volunteer work and my drum circles, which were attended monthly by an average of 200 people. I hadn't applied to speak. Ironically, hundreds of other applicants did, yet I was the one chosen.

I soon found myself standing on stage, facing an audience of 10,000 people, my words being broadcast to one hundred nations across the world, looking into the floodlights and a sea of faces, I was in awe being there. Before taking the stage, as the microphone was pinned onto my dress, my body shook with fear. "Who am I? Why should people listen to me?" I wondered. I wanted to hide, to be the wallflower. But I knew I was put on that stage for a reason- not for a message from me, but for a message delivered *through* me. My ego told me to run and hide. My humility kept me planted and willing to serve.

I never sought the stage; the opportunity was there because I had spent years serving, wanting to make the world a little better, and learning to push past shyness through sales training. I was content to be in the shadows, but light flooded upon me. Whatever reason I was chosen, I knew I had the responsibility to do my absolute best and deliver the message confidently, the way that the message deserved to be. The best way to serve was to show up with courage.

My toes were on the edge of the stage. Just like they were at the edge of the cobblestone on the day when I called to rent the building on Main Street to create a place for healing and education.

I had prepared daily for that moment, not knowing I was. Being true to myself, working with grit and tenacity, striving to improve every day while putting one foot in front of the other. Making the best of the cards dealt to me. "Luck," some would say.

CHAPTER TEN

Jasmine Nesbitt

Jasmine Nesbitt Real Estate Investing

Real Estate Investor and Mentor

@blackmarketre

CREATING HER EMPIRE

Jasmine's journey is one of resilience, determination, and unwavering ambition. Born into poverty and surrounded by family struggles with addiction, Jasmine refused to let her circumstances define her future. Enduring frequent hardships, including periods without electricity, water, and scarcity of food, this ignited a fervent resolve within her to break free from adversity's cycle and carve out a better life.

In the face of adversity, Jasmine learned a fundamental truth: there is always a solution and hard work can conquer any obstacle. Her relentless drive and refusal to accept defeat propelled her forward, even when the odds seemed insurmountable.

After weathering the storm of divorce and shouldering the weight of supporting her family, Jasmine reached a turning point. Exhausted and burnt out, she knew she needed a change. Drawing upon her skills and passion for real estate, Jasmine embarked on a journey to pursue her dreams and provide a better future for herself and her children.

Driven by an unyielding commitment to her goals, Jasmine refused to settle for mediocrity. Her journey is a testament to the power of perseverance and the belief that with the right mindset, anyone can achieve greatness.

Live Your Dream Life Now

◆

By Jasmine Nesbitt

Bang! The gun went off, and all our bodies went running out fast to get in a good position. Bang bang! We were called back. Someone had fallen in the first 100 meters, so it's an automatic call back to give everyone a fair chance at the race. We get lined up again, nerves even higher from the callback. Guns up, bang! Off I go again; this start was even better than the last. I find myself in the lead pack with the top women in the nation. I hear my coach yell to relax and pace myself. I relaxed a little, and I found women passing me. Halfway through the race, I found myself mentally checked out and hurting. I had let a teammate get close to me that I had beaten all season. I was on the struggle bus but had to make a choice, and I wouldn't let them pass me. My coach said to just catch two girls. I sat there and checked back in. I already hurt, so I decided to let it hurt. One girl, two girls, three girls! I didn't have a lot of space left in the race, so I just kept chasing. Sprinting down the finish, wanting that top 40 and knowing I am just giving my all, passing another girl to the finish line. I had caught six girls by the finish! I cooled down and waited for the results.

This was my freshman year of college. I was warming up for the regional cross-country championships with my team. I was nervous but excited. The kind of nervous that I knew I was shooting for something out of my league, and I was prepared to get what I wanted. It had already been achieved mentally for me. I wanted to go to Nationals, but I knew there were many older and better women than me; top 40 was the goal, and it was lofty, but I wanted it, and I had the drive and mentality to go for it. With 20 teams and over 130 women in the field, many of those teams and women are set to be the best of the best in the nation! I was supposed to be around 60th place based on the season results. I had been the top runner for my team that season, and realistically, from my training, I should not have been. They trained year-round, and I found myself balancing training and chronic injuries. I did my best during practices and races but didn't train as often as my teammates. "How do you do it? What do you do? I just don't get it. You perform so well, and that's great, but it doesn't make sense. Run us through what you do." My teammate asked while warming up.

I said, "Well, it's easy. I have been imagining this race with any possible outcome and how I would react to all those possibilities, so whatever happens, I am prepared and already know my response to it." I had done that for every race I knew I would be in and planned every outcome, prioritizing winning them every time, whether that was realistic or not. I knew what I wanted, so I made it happen. Going to bed, I would play it through in my head over and over, making those my realities, and then it would play out in real life. So I guided them through it. I went over the start of the race and how I would run straight on the tangent and get out hard. Then there were little hills that I would keep my cadence on and power down, then cut right for the shortest route to ensure I wasn't running extra distance to my kick at the finish. I told them I had been mentally going over this race for weeks already. The results came in, and I came in 38th place. I did it! 38th place out of the top women in the nation!

Throughout my career, I realized this was why I was better than most and won most of the races I was in despite injuries and training differences. I was mentally tough; I had manifested all of it before, and I accepted the pain that came with what I wanted. That was the only thing I could tell that set me apart from the other women who were not injured and were training more consistently than me. Throughout my athletic career, people would ask the same questions about how I compete so well, considering everything. They knew I should not be doing that well, which always came back to those three things.

I accepted that it would be hard mentally, and I had to choose what hardships I wanted in life. My mentality is to manifest and imagine the results I want as if they were my reality at that moment. I accepted that getting to that point would hurt physically, and I had to embrace it rather than fight it. This had been true for everything in my life; I just hadn't realized it until later. I have manifested and visualized my life to be what I wanted, and when things didn't go as planned, I had to make those hard decisions, stay mentally strong, and push through the pain to keep going and get the desired results.

The great thing is that anyone can do this! The unfortunate thing is that most will not. People don't like to be uncomfortable and in pain. Most people can't handle it and settle for what is most comfortable, whether emotional, mental, physical, or other. The easiest path forward they will choose for their life. This is what separates normal individuals and successful individuals. It makes sense that individuals dislike being in pain or uncomfortable situations. The unknown can be scary, and fear can take over and make someone complacent. It's easy for someone to want to stay in the known and normal of life even if they are unhappy and desire more. Which one are you?

You need to accept these truths to start implementing them in your life. That you are being complacent and not living the life you want. Life is hard either way. It is hard to stay complacent when you are miserable and unhappy. It is also hard to work towards the life you want to live. One just leads to the possibility of a happier life. Your brain doesn't know the difference between truth and lies, reality and imagination. What you see, think, and hear are all truths to your brain. You need to visualize who you want to be and how you want to live and surround yourself with those people. Manifesting brings the right energies and ideas to your life, but you will stay in the same place if you don't act with those. All of this is to transform you into the person you want to be. The person who takes action is the person who makes hard decisions that lead them to what they want. That person is there; you just have to unleash it from the fear, complacency, people telling you what you have is enough, and the what-ifs in life.

You decide what is enough in your life. What if life is so much more than you can even imagine? Fear is a figment of your imagination, and so are the what-ifs'. They are holding you back from what is arguably the most important part: taking action. Take action to at least have the chance to live a life you love. I used this in my life, not perfectly, but with effort through the highs and lows. This allowed me to leave the life of poverty my family had and get a higher education completely paid for. This allowed me to leave my abusive marriage and start living my life the way I wanted and provide for my three wonderful children. This allowed me to strive for more and create the life I want. All through those three things.

While it can seem daunting and overwhelming, you can sometimes implement this in your life. Start with accepting those three truths, then take action. It doesn't have to be perfect, but movement forward is still movement forward. This is your life, and at the end of the day, what happens is all your decisions regarding what you allow and accept in your life. You need to accept better things. Life is amazing, and we are so lucky to have the option to make our lives precisely what we want. It is going to be mentally challenging, it is going to be physically uncomfortable, and you will have to accept your hardships in life, but I promise you can do it. Every successful individual you look up to is a human who has made hard decisions just like you. You can create the life you deserve even if you're not living it right now. Will you take action to live your dream life?

CHAPTER ELEVEN

Christina Haws
Real Estate Agent for Real Broker, LLC

@bosshawsinvestments
https://www.facebook.com/christina.haws.90
https://www.linkedin.com/in/christina-haws-7a1939152/

Christina Haws has a Bachelor's Degree from the University of Utah. She enjoys hiking and exploring new places with her family, which includes her husband, Robert, and their 4 kids. She enjoys exercising, gardening, and making salsa!

Four years ago, Christina began learning about real estate investing and became hooked! She has since flipped three houses, done a few wholesale deals, got involved in property management, and purchased & operated rental properties. She and her husband own a small mobile home and RV Park. She has a special fascination for purchasing deals with seller financing. She recently got her real estate license. Christina and Robert created their business LLC called Boss Haws Investments. As Robert likes to say, "Christina is the Boss, and I am the Haws."

It Takes Grit!

By Christina Haws

In the Fall of 2019, I became acquainted with the Bigger Pockets Podcast and started listening to it. I soon recognized the wealth of information offered there and started devouring each "episode" as if I were in college again. I discovered that you can be a real estate investor without much money. I gleaned that it was possible to do this through learning, perseverance, and grit - lots of grit.

The first investment strategy we implemented was renting out our primary residence and moving into my parent's house. Next, we purchased a house to fix up and do the BRRRR (Buy, Rehab, Rent, Refinance, and Repeat) method. We hired a handyman to do most of the rehab for us. We paid him the full agreed-upon amount before the project was finished. Unfortunately, that didn't go as well as we had hoped, and we had to fire him. We had to find a new contractor and ended up paying the second one even more than the first to fix the problems the first guy created. After fixing the house, we opted to sell it rather than rent it. We would have lost money in a regular market, but the silver lining was that the market had appreciated since the time of purchase (9 months earlier), so we could come out on top.

Lessons learned: always vet your contractors! Do not pay them before things have been completed. Always over-calculate on the rehab costs and have reserves on hand. Each deal might not be a home run but it gives you experience (grit) and makes you stronger and smarter for the next deal.

While we were doing the house flip, I joined a real estate/wholesaling apprenticeship program. I became aware of a mobile home park for sale by the owner. I started calling other mobile home parks nearby to get an idea of comparables. I called the park owner of Shady Acres Mobile Home and RV Park and asked about rental rates. I asked if they might be interested in selling the park during our conversation. They commented that they *were indeed* interested in selling the park. My heart skipped a beat with excitement when I heard this. I asked if they would consider seller financing on the property, and they said, "Yes." By now, I was screaming inside with elation. Was this real? This was an off-market property with income opportunities *and* seller financing!

Later that day, I approached my husband about this park called Shady Acres. I told him we should buy this park as an investment property. He said, "We don't know how to run a mobile home/RV park, we've never done something like that before. It's not just an investment, it's a business." I said, "I know, you are right, but this could be a *good* deal and we will figure it out as we go."

With the sellers, we agreed upon a down payment, a purchase price, a monthly payment with no interest, and a 10-year term loan with a balloon payment due at the end. We purchased the park in October 2021. We have worked on improving the physical appearance and infrastructure of the park, updating the homes, getting a new sign, advertising it online, and creating a website (www.shadyacreshuntington.com). At this point, we are three years in, and have learned that you sometimes have to have thick skin (grit) in dealing with tenants, managers, and RV site visitors while maintaining a sense of humor and humility. We are excited about the potential of this investment in the future.

In October 2023, I had a routine mammogram. The radiologist felt there were some areas that looked suspicious on my right side, so he requested I come back for a breast biopsy. Three days after the biopsy, I received a phone call from the radiologist telling me I had breast cancer. When you receive a phone call like that, it is hard to process everything they tell you. My first thought was: "Wait, what? Did you just say I have *breast cancer*? I'm too young for breast cancer." Surgery? Already?" It was challenging to focus on everything they were instructing me to do. They told me to get an MRI scheduled and to make an appointment with a surgeon!

The following month was spent researching surgeons, getting my breast MRI, and digesting the information about the type of cancer I had. I told my husband, " I don't have time for cancer." He chuckled and said, "If it means saving your life, we *will make time* for it!" One gal that I spoke with who had dealt with breast cancer told me how she chose to stay positive through the whole ordeal. I liked her mantra! It would be easy to fall into the trap of saying, 'Poor me,' why me? I'm just going to have a pity party for myself.' Instead, I resigned myself to having a positive outlook about my condition, continuing to exercise to be my strongest and face this head-on. Just like real estate investing, this was going to take some grit. I envisioned myself getting rid of the cancer, and I prayed hard for help. I knew I could beat it! I chose the attitude of 'What can I learn from this' rather than 'Why me'? My sweet sister sent me pink boxing gloves with the message, "You are a fighter! You got this!" That was it! I was going to fight this and overcome it!

It was determined that I would need to have a unilateral (right side) mastectomy and 5 axillary (armpit area) lymph nodes removed. The surgery required both a general surgeon and a plastic surgeon. I had the surgery on January 4, 2024. I came home the same day with my chest wrapped up tightly like a burrito and with a drain inserted in my side. I went for a post-surgery follow-up four days later at the plastic surgeon's office. This was the first time I saw myself after surgery with the bandages removed, I thought the site looked like a Star Wars character!

I had weekly follow-up visits for eight weeks, monitoring my progress, making sure there were no infections, and preparing for reconstruction. It is amazing what modern medicine can do now; in some ways, it was a fascinating process. It was also comical at times with the jokes my husband and I made along the way. It helped things feel lighter and make the best of the situation. Jokes such as 'Well, at least you get to be the size that you always wanted' and "Going through the big "C" and I don't mean Connecticut, we're gonna fight it and get rid of it" (sung to the tune of 'Going Through the Big D, and I Don't Mean Dallas' by Mark Chestnut)

During this time, I met with the Oncologist twice, and on the second visit, I received news that my "Onco Score" (a test used to measure the risk of cancer recurrence) was low, and that meant *I DID NOT have to do chemotherapy or radiation*!!! My husband and I cheered with relief and gave thanks for answered prayers!

This was such great news! I got to keep my hair, I could continue to heal and get strong!

When writing this, it has been 10 weeks since surgery. The plan for me now is to continue to heal and prepare for reconstruction surgery in approximately 6 months.

Going through this experience, I realized that everything was not sunshine and rainbows, and there were discomforts and challenges. I had friends telling me, 'You are so strong,' and I said that I didn't see myself as strong, but I knew I had to deal with it head-on and face it. A friend responded, "Sometimes we don't see things about ourselves that others can see." We ALL are strong and can do hard things!

I had set a goal to get my real estate license before I learned I had cancer. I kept on with my goal and worked on my real estate schooling while recovering from surgery. Once I found out I didn't need to have further cancer treatment, it helped spur me to get the schooling done quicker. I have now passed the real estate exam and am a real estate agent.

Life will always give us unexpected challenges, but we need not to let those challenges derail us from achieving our goals. Adversity can be a transformative power, it teaches us patience, grit, humility, and faith. It's through these trials that we often find our greatest opportunities for growth, and self-discovery, and become more empathetic and charitable to others.

As M.H. Clark said: "Your life is still a story of joy and complexity, trial and overcoming." Now, remember to get your annual mammograms!

CHAPTER TWELVE

Samantha Woodward
Real Estate Essentials
Realtor

https://linktr.ee/samanthawoodwardrealtor

Samantha Benedict Woodward resides in Eagle Mountain, Utah, with her husband and three wonderful children. Together, they run a thriving real estate investment business, with Samantha excelling as a Realtor. Her passion for helping others extends beyond her professional endeavors, empowering women to pursue their dreams. Samantha's journey is a testament to resilience, determination, and the pursuit of excellence in both personal and professional realms. Her commitment to continuous growth and learning fuels her drive to make a positive impact on the lives of those around her, leaving a lasting legacy of inspiration and empowerment.

The Ray of Sunshine Rekindled

By Samantha Woodward

My journey has been filled with dazzling light and deep shadows. It's the story of a curious, joyful girl who lost her inner spark and fought back to reclaim her radiant spirit. I'm not just a successful businesswoman; I'm a survivor, a woman who found purpose and strength in the face of darkness.

As a child, I was a ray of sunshine. A thirst for knowledge fueled endless questions and explorations. My non-stop questions often tested the limits of my mother's patience, but I could not resist the urge to unravel the mysteries of the world around me. My beloved grandmother was my guiding light, nurturing my self-worth and spirit. We'd cherish the simplest moments - giggling over silly TV shows like The Golden Girls, sharing secrets while painting our nails, or making homemade chocolate chip cookies just to eat the cookie dough. Her love was a warm, unwavering presence.

Her passing of cancer when I was ten shattered my world. Lost in grief, I craved connection. Friendships were a lifeline, but secretly, I ached for something deeper. Sadly, my parents were overwhelmed by their own struggles, leaving me feeling adrift. Superficial bonds became my substitute for the unconditional love I'd lost. Worst of all, past sexual abuse, a shameful secret, poisoned my self-esteem. Ironically, I began to blame the very quality that drew others to me—my sunny disposition. Was it the catalyst to attract the darkness that exploited me? Walls arose, and the vibrant girl I once was gradually faded into the background behind them. Moving to Park City should have been a fresh start, but my inner light flickered. Unhealthy relationships became my norm, fueled by my own unhealed wounds. In response to my mother's concern and the visible distress caused by my loss, therapy became a comforting source of solace and support. Alongside therapy, I started keeping a personal journal. Its pages became a sanctuary where I could pour out my heart, unraveling the tangled threads of grief and finding my path forward, but my deepest secret remained buried. It dimmed my shine.

During middle and high school, I navigated through a multitude of friend groups in pursuit of a sense of belonging and purpose. This journey ultimately led me to join the cheerleading team in high school, which provided a degree of fulfillment, but I still yearned for a deeper level of acceptance and connection. Upon graduating, I pursued a career in massage therapy with aspirations of becoming a doctor. My initial plan was to perform daily massages and use the earnings to self-fund medical school. However, unexpectedly, massage therapy satisfied my desire to help others and offered the flexibility of hours and the potential for income that aligned with my future goal of starting a family. I have embraced a lifelong journey of learning and personal growth throughout my life. This quest has taken me through diverse educational experiences, including massage therapy, emergency medicine, cosmetology, and real estate. But even with this success, an unquenchable yearning burned within.

Driven by the pain of lost love, I entered a hasty marriage, believing it could mend my broken heart. However, the marriage plunged me deeper into darkness as I confronted his betrayal and addiction. Amidst the despair, a flicker of inner strength persisted. With newfound determination, I broke free from the toxic situation and sought solace in therapy. This journey of self-discovery helped me delve into the roots of my pain, leading to growth and healing. During this transformative journey, I uncovered the detrimental effects of my secret and the reasons behind my endurance of toxic relationships. Slowly, I began to heal. Upon finding myself, love entered my life like a beacon. My supportive partner has stood unwavering as my pillar of strength, offering unwavering patience and empathy while we navigate through the intricacies of my lingering fears and emotional triggers. Though motherhood was fulfilling, the woman who'd dreamt of making a big impact on the world remained restless. In an unexpected twist of fate, my career flourished in the realm of finance. Guiding clients through complex financial landscapes brought me a profound sense of purpose. The challenges and novelty inherent in my role, especially in facilitating global real estate acquisitions, instilled a renewed sense of independence and self-identity. This empowering experience led me to a realization that I had finally discovered my true calling in life.

2008 marked a devastating moment in my life. The revelation that the real estate investment company I was affiliated with was a fraudulent Ponzi scheme shattered my financial landscape. This tumultuous period was further compounded when the chiropractor I worked alongside experienced a mental crisis and attempted to orchestrate an explosion at our workplace in a deliberate act of insurance fraud. Fortunately, the dentist in the office above our suite discovered the gas cans before any harm could occur. These unfortunate events abruptly ended my massage therapy practice and my financial career.

Navigating family life, losing material possessions, and juggling the demands of work and motherhood shaped my perspective on what truly matters. Cosmetology school provided a creative outlet, allowing me to be a hands-on mother to my young children. This experience allowed me to successfully balance my professional and personal roles, creating a fulfilling and harmonious lifestyle.

As my oldest daughter approached her tenth birthday, I noticed striking similarities to my own struggles at that age. She expressed profound feelings of depression and hopelessness, which deeply resonated with me. Resolute in my purpose to support her unwaveringly, I devoted substantial time to ensure she received professional therapy, mindful of its positive impact during my teenage years. During this period, I serendipitously discovered the transformative Emotion Code technique, which became an invaluable tool in our shared healing journey.

Juggling multiple roles as a massage therapist, cosmetologist, and mother, I felt profound gratitude. However, I also recognized that I needed to assume a more substantial financial responsibility to provide a stable foundation for my family. Moreover, I found myself yearning for a more fulfilling and challenging path. Being the ambitious individual in my relationship, I felt a strong obligation to secure our family's future. The desire to re-enter the real estate industry became increasingly irresistible.

Living in a state of perpetual anxiety, where the fight-or-flight response dominated my mind, and the fear of judgment loomed constantly, I was unable to savor life's precious moments fully. My perception of my relationship with my husband, initially viewed as positive, underwent a shift. Reflecting on my past relationship, I recognized my husband's remarkable support, kindness, and paternal qualities. However, his tendency to avoid conflicts often left me feeling guilty for advocating for myself or our children, unwittingly contributing to my unhappiness. I felt suffocated, unable to express my true voice and fulfill my potential.

The well-intentioned efforts of my husband to "protect" me were unknowingly stifling my personal growth. Boundaries, instead of being a form of control, were an act of self-love. The walls I had erected to survive had inadvertently blocked the joy I yearned for. It was time to let my inner light shine through, breaking free from these self-imposed restrictions. Therapy revealed hidden cracks in my seemingly happy marriage, revealing subtle dynamics masked by my dominant nature. While my husband meant well, his desire to shield me had inadvertently stifled my growth. Boundaries were not a weapon but an act of self-love, and the walls built for survival had also blocked the joy I craved. It was time to let my inner light shine through truly.

My story is proof that even deep scars can mend. I choose my shine, fueled by confidence and a relentless drive to create a fulfilling legacy. It's OK – even essential – for women to dream big! My past may have shaped me, but it won't define me.

Grand dreams need a map – write your goals down and create vision boards! Surround yourself with positive people and mentors. And never be afraid to seek help on your path. Motherhood and fierce ambition can beautifully coexist.

Embrace your amazing journey, triumphs, and hardships. Let negativity bounce off you, protect your heart, and let your brilliance illuminate the world. Each stumble is a chance to grow stronger. When the voice of doubt whispers, respond with a roar: "Watch me!"

In the realm of obscurity, navigating your path to radiance requires profound self-awareness and the unwavering courage to confront the shadows of the past. Embrace the scars of your journey, recognizing their potential to heal and transform who you are. Take stock of your present moment, acknowledging your fears and aspirations, for it is the foundation for your future direction. Ignite your path with unwavering self-belief, becoming a beacon of inspiration for others. Dare to dream audaciously, shattering limitations and embarking on a voyage of self-discovery. Through introspection and restorative practices, uncover your true essence and manifest your grandest aspirations. Design a life that surpasses even your wildest dreams. Let your inner light radiate, illuminating the world with your innate worth and resilience. Remember, every stumble is a stepping stone toward a remarkable transformation. Embrace your journey, and let your light guide you on this transformative path.

CHAPTER THIRTEEN

Noa Bel

Success Coach

@noabel_coach
@thenoabel

CREATING HER EMPIRE

Noa Bel, an empowerment, success and spiritual life coach, with over two decades worth of experience, has dedicated her life (and continues to do so) to help others master their mindset and create more prosperity, happiness and inner peace. That's where her true passion lies - in helping those who are in search of their own voice and purpose in life.

With her knowledge and compassionate heart, Noa has helped guide thousands of women and men from all walks of life to realize their God-given potential on their way to live far more fulfilling lives, aided by three powerful ancient practices that she has spent years exploring and studying Feng shui, Kabbalah numerology, and astrology.

These life-changing tools have also helped Noa herself on her journey to find her true self and connect with the divine, and she considers it her life's mission to share and teach others about these treasured ancient gifts, firmly believing that everyone should be aware of the incredible power that they hold.

In Noa's own words, "Spirituality is a compass, guiding us through life's ups and downs. It is a journey, not a destination.

Weathering Storms

by Noa Bel

What doesn't kill...

Louisa May Alcott's wise words, "I am not afraid of storms, for I am learning how to sail my ship," have been spinning in my head for years now, ever since I first stumbled upon this famous quote by the 'little women' author. It resonates so deeply within me because I too often feel that the many storms I have weathered throughout my life have made me the woman I am today. Over time, I've come to welcome and embrace these 'storms' for I know they're always teaching me valuable lessons and offering me greater insight into myself. It is thanks to them that I'm a much stronger person. It has taken me a while, but I now better understand what Nietzsche meant by saying, 'What doesn't kill you makes you stronger. '

Life is a Casino

With time, I've adapted a gambler's approach to life and nowadays try to take far more risks, calculated risks but risks nonetheless. It gets the blood pumping in my veins and helps connect me to my inner child, vibrating my soul with youthful energy. I've learned that it's okay to make mistakes or suffer losses in pursuing big wins, just like in a casino. These days, I dread words like 'safety' and 'stability,' for they spell death to me. A flatline is never a good thing, whether in a hospital when one's hooked to a machine or in life. As long as I keep learning and growing, no matter how often I fall flat on my face, I know I'm on the right track. And that is what this inspirational quote by Miss Alcott is all about - the value of learning. Every day, each of us learns how to steer our ship. And that's enough. We don't need more than that. But that's also the hard part - accepting that learning is *enough*.

I Am Born

But I should start right from the beginning, or from my very humble beginning - I was born in Be'er Sheva, a biblical town of southern Israel - a desert city that serves as a gateway to the Negev region. My brother and I grew up in a relatively modest environment, raised by my hardworking parents. Even though money was tight in those days, we never lacked a thing. My wonderful parents made sure of that. But I was also very much aware of how hard they worked, living from paycheck to paycheck, and I remember making a promise to myself very young that I would have financial freedom as an adult. Even as a teenage girl I had already dreamed of carving out a successful career in either banking or finance. And that's exactly what came to pass.

A Gilded Cage

As soon as I was released from the Israeli army in 1996, where I had served as a combat medic, I started working at Bank Leumi in Israel and, at the same time, graduated with a bachelor's degree in economics and management. I passed the management tests at the bank and became a manager of the entire Shephelah region's business sector. Those were pleasant times for me. Not only was I on my way to fulfilling my dream of becoming financially secure, but I had also married my first husband, Michael, with whom I had my two daughters - Dorin and Lian. I foolishly believed I had it all. But a gilded cage is still a cage, which is what my work at the bank was. There wasn't much room for either innovation or flexibility in that line of work. Something I had secretly craved but couldn't bring myself to admit I needed. But life has a way of unfolding in mysterious ways, often leading us down unexpected paths.

A Sense of Calling

In 2001, when Dorin was two years old, Michael and I lived in a high-rise building on the 16th floor, and one evening, we had a terrible fight and decided to get a divorce. Come morning, Michael got up for work and, at around 6 am, had already left the apartment, absentmindedly locking the front door from the outside. Dorin and I were both still tucked in our beds and soundly asleep, each in her room. At a certain point, I awakened momentarily from a fitful sleep and caught a glimpse of smoke from under our bedroom door. I figured this was just a dream and went back to sleep, but then, I suddenly heard the most blood-curdling scream and quickly realized it was my daughter's voice. I instantly shot out of bed, opened our bedroom door, and saw smoke everywhere. I fearlessly pierced through that wall of smoke and made it to my daughter's room, taking her in my arms and trying to soothe her. It was so dark I couldn't even tell whether it was day or night. I somehow managed to reach the front door, carrying Dorin in my arms, and realized that Michael had locked the door with the key nowhere in sight! My heart sank to my stomach! I started banging on the door, screaming for help, but none of the neighbors heard my angry calls. I felt so powerless, so helpless, thinking this must be some horrific nightmare. I sat on a nearby chair, tightly holding on to Dorin, and prayed to God, begging him to help us in our most desperate hour. And then the strangest thing happened. I suddenly had the most startling vision flashing before my stunned eyes - that of myself as a very young girl, surrounded by three other children I knew to be my siblings. All four of us were trapped in a blazing fire that raged across our home. A man, whom I recognized as my father, came through our room's door and started lifting us one by one, shuffling us through the open window to the adjacent balcony, where it was much safer. The startling part was that this girl looked nothing like me! And lord knows I have only one brother! At that moment, I realized I had somehow conjured up a memory from a past life! "The balcony! That's it!" I heard myself whispering, grabbed my daughter without a moment's hesitation, and ran amok toward our balcony. We miraculously made it there, and that's the last thing I remember since both Dorin and I passed out when we reached the balcony.

Later, at the hospital, I learned exactly what had happened from that moment on. Shortly after we had lost consciousness, the firefighters found us, and we were rushed to a nearby hospital. As it turned out, the neighbor in the apartment right below ours had her AC on throughout the night while its motor was near her clothesline. There was a short circuit due to friction with the wet clothes, and everything caught fire. Our entire apartment went up in flames and got burnt. We lost all our possessions. The fire postponed our divorce, and we moved into a temporary apartment, finding ourselves for the first time in a long while in a rather dire financial state as we awaited the insurance money. But I didn't care - I knew it was a miracle that we got out of that fire alive and felt nothing but the utmost gratitude to God for saving me and my daughter. Whatever that strange and indescribable vision was, I knew God was behind it.

The Wheel of Change

A couple of weeks later, I returned to my work at the bank but couldn't shake this inexplicable feeling in the pit of my stomach that my life would never be the same again after that experience. It stirred up something within me, something I couldn't possibly ignore. I had so many questions, yet so few answers. I knew one thing, though—my life was about to undergo a serious change.

I began seeking spiritual guidance in hopes someone would help shed light on the experience, finding myself sitting across several psychics, tarot card readers, and healers. I became more and more fascinated by all things spiritual, reading everything I possibly could find online, especially about reincarnation. One thing led to another, and I soon came across the ancient Chinese practice of Feng shui, which centers around energy flow and teaches how to invite abundance into your life by arranging living and working spaces. I was instantly hooked. I signed up for a course and loved every minute, applying the things I learned in my immediate surroundings - at the office and at home. And heaven behold, it worked like a charm! A couple of weeks later, I was offered a promotion at the bank, and the insurance money Michael and I so anxiously expected finally went through. I was floored by how quickly this practice has proven itself. This led to several more courses, chief among them courses in numerology and astrology. Before I knew it, I began counseling friends and family members, empowering and helping them navigate the challenges they encountered in all areas of life, using these fabulous new tools I now had at my disposal. I've learned that nothing gives me greater joy than helping and inspiring others on this awesome life journey, aiding them to realize their God-given potential. As far as I'm concerned, these ancient practices are lifesavers. They've certainly changed and saved mine. They say that 'one needs to give up all to achieve all," and that's precisely what I did. I resigned from the bank and began devoting all my time and energy to deepening my studies in these fields while slowly and gradually turning this newfound love into a profession. Before I knew it, I was already offering my spiritual guidance skills to hundreds and hundreds of people from all walks of life, building a strong client base in Israel.

The world is Your Oyster.

Years later, in 2020, I did it again and shuffled the cards of my life. A voice inside me said: "Noa, you must step out of your comfort zone, pack up your bags, and relocate yourself abroad. For now, your work in Israel is done, and it's time for you to share your gifts with the world". And I listened. A dear friend of mine had just put down roots in Florida, and I jumped on the chance of joining him there and treating myself to a once-in-a-lifetime adventure while leaving family and friends behind in Israel. Two days after my arrival, I kid you not, I met my beloved future husband David, and we had already married within six months!

I've been in the States for almost five years now - happily married and coaching/giving spiritual counsel to women and men from all over the world, not just the States: Canada, Australia, London, Germany, and more...Guiding and advising those who struggle to tread through life's trials and many obstacles. Not only that, I've also begun sharing the knowledge I've acquired on social media, Instagram in particular. Within a year, I have already reached millions of views and over 100,000 followers, and these numbers keep growing...

Listen to that little voice inside you - it never lies...

CHAPTER FOURTEEN

Vivienne Pierre

You Unleashed (Owner)

Physical Therapist/ Real Estate Investor/Coach

https://linktr.ee/ViviennePierre
https://www.facebook.com/vlpierre
https://www.instagram.com/trini_doc/

Access your Free D.R.I.V.E assessment at
https://www.discoveryourdrive.com/76119/home

CREATING HER EMPIRE

Vivienne, originally from Trinidad & Tobago, infuses her vibrant Caribbean spirit with her. Transitioning from a part-time Doctor of Physical Therapy ex National Volleyball Player to a successful real estate investor and entrepreneur, Vivienne couldn't be confined by a traditional job. Discovering her true potential through the DRIVE system, she altered her financial path and embraced a life of continuous self-improvement. Known for her high energy, charisma, and innovative approach, Vivienne excels in the face of both victory and defeat. Her resilience and determination have not only shaped her life but equipped her to empower others. With a combination of learned skill sets, toolsets, and mindsets, she assists clients in designing their lives to turn dreams into reality. Vivienne uses her unique strengths and experiences with her unwavering commitment to impact lives. She ensures that she isn't just building an empire for herself—she's helping others create their dream empires, too.

Courage Beyond Borders: A Path To Freedom

By Vivienne Pierre

Roots and Rebellion: A Personal Awakening

In the heart of Trinidad and Tobago (T&T), where the Caribbean sun blesses the land with its eternal warmth, I, the only girl and the second of three children, was born to a medical doctor and teacher. My upbringing was imprinted upon my nation's transformation from a colonial past to Independence in 1962 and a Republic in 1976. This experiment crafted a vision for education that profoundly influenced my family's ethos and, unknowingly, my path.

As an introverted girl, where societal norms expected children to be seen and not heard, I found my voice on the volleyball court. This became my sanctuary, where I could truly be… myself. By 18, I was the captain of the Under 21 T&T National Volleyball Team, using the sport not just as a game but as a platform for expression and achievement. My rebellion against societal norms whispered, "Stay in your place."

In 1999, I traded the indoor and sandy courts of T&T for the vast, unpredictable world beyond the Caribbean Sea to the United States of America. It was an odyssey of the soul driven by an insatiable curiosity and a passion that burned red hot. Volleyball had instilled in me the art of resilience—the ability to leap, land firmly, and rise again, regardless of how tumultuous or unpredictable the fall. These were qualities that would inevitably help me navigate a world vastly different from the one I had known for so long.

Bridging Continents and Cultures

I was fluent in hard work and quickly learned about the challenges of living as part of the new middle class in the USA. I was Dr. Vivienne Pierre, an esteemed Doctor of Physical Therapy, but financial stability remained elusive. The dream of success and the equation supposedly defined by hard work equaling success seemed a mirage. I faced the harsh reality of living paycheck to paycheck, a narrative far too familiar in what was supposed to be the land of opportunity.

I would build my nest egg, then, POOF- in an instant, it would be gone. I was allocating money to my savings, investments like a matched 401k plan and disability insurance, like *they* said I should. I still had more bills than money at the end of the month. For how many of us is this the reality? The financial rollercoaster of the middle class—with its high taxes, high costs, and exorbitant healthcare bills—left me and many others reeling. This reality affected more individuals than I ever thought possible, and it challenged my understanding of economic success in America.

You could say I was surviving, but like so many others, I was also suffering in silence!

Grief and Resilience: Redefining Freedom

The turning point in my life came unexpectedly and painfully with the loss of my mother on August 26, 2013, a day after my birthday. My mother, a woman of great faith, tradition, and openness, had significantly impacted our community as a teacher and was my #1 supporter. The loss of a parent is always a tough pill to swallow. But for me, this was a storm that no amount of resilience could initially weather. Having my job be jeopardized based on my decision to return to Trinidad before my mom's untimely death was a decision that would forever be etched as a defining moment in my life. It led to my new definition of Freedom - having the autonomy to prioritize life without the looming threat of loss.

The invincible athlete, the unstoppable force, the conqueror, faced the one opponent she couldn't outmaneuver: GRIEF. This pivotal moment galvanized my resolve to never again let external circumstances dictate my ability to care for my loved ones.

The Mirage of the American Dream: Confronting Economic Realities

Amid the turmoil, I decisively shifted toward entrepreneurship, a move driven by deep introspection and the understanding that mental resilience is as crucial as a financial strategy. Driven by a newfound clarity, I embarked on a journey of self-investment. My engagement with the Woody Woodward D.R.I.V.E personality assessment revealed that I had primary "Relator" and secondary "Intellect" traits. This insight explained my deep-seated need for family, relationships, influence, connection, and a zest for knowledge and understanding. Included in this was a tendency toward over-analysis, often stalling and hindering decisive action.

My mind was a whirlwind of thoughts, but through visualization and daily gratitude, I gained clearer insights, understanding that bold implementation of my plans was vital. Along with the D.R.I.V.E system, Neuro-Linguistic Programming (NLP) became a transformative tool, reshaping my thought patterns and empowering me to override the limiting beliefs that had confined my potential. "I am not good enough" and "I don't have what it takes to be successful" were transformed into "I am a master of my finances and deserving of success." These mental shifts, facilitated by a deeper dive into the D.R.I.V.E system, helped me escape the paralysis of analysis, steering me towards a life where passion and self-worth became central.

Turning Point: Embracing Entrepreneurship

Facing my limitations, I acknowledged my lack of the necessary skills, tools, and mindset to elevate myself to the next level. My past thinking had constrained me to my existing level of success. It necessitated a conscious decision to invest in my mental growth and gain alignment with my secondary D.R.I.V.E. Recognizing that my mindset traveled with me everywhere led to the realization that mental excellence is the precursor to taking the necessary actions to achieve one's dreams. Immersing myself in a community of diverse, like-minded individuals was what I needed for continuous learning and adaptability. Even as an accomplished Doctor of Physical Therapy, I had to be open to discovering my blind spots and ready for the occasional reality check… a.k.a a swift kick in the you-know-where, when it mattered!

It's true! Resilience isn't how often you get knocked down but how often you rise and keep moving forward. I have felt the nausea of the rollercoaster ride of failure. From not securing a desired job as a therapist or the loss as a Head coach and National player. Even as a real estate investor with a failed deal or one that required that I pivot along the way. The important thing is that irrespective of my circumstances, I decided to STAY IN THE GAME, driven by my enduring commitment to being one step closer to creating my dream empire!

In times of stumbles and falls, the credit does not belong to the critic. It belongs to the one in the arena whose battle scars are the stain of sweat and blood. My new adventure was never one of a cold and timid soul. I savor and experience victory and defeat.

Those so-called failures became learning lessons and stepping stones to thousands of dollars saved in taxes, opportunities to speak in front of national players, future investors, business owners, and rehabilitation professionals, with moments that help shape the therapists of tomorrow's generation. Staying in the game helped me alter my financial trajectory by completing twelve real estate investing transactions and counting towards generational wealth. Traveling to spend time with family, more than I have ever been able to do, became non-negotiable. Even to create cash flow during COVID times when great financial insecurity and instability existed. I continued to grow and became the person I needed to be to keep building my dream empire!

The Journey of Personal Investment and Community

The quest for success is an individual odyssey defined by personal aspirations and the resilience to transform failure into opportunity. My evolution from a national volleyball player to head coach, then a Doctor of Physical Therapy, and finally a successful entrepreneur, highlights the enduring value of perseverance and self-belief. Guided by the insights from the D.R.I.V.E system and leveraging other educational tools in my arsenal, each career phase has deepened my self-awareness, honed my communication skills, and taught me to use every challenge as a growth opportunity. This understanding has enabled me to navigate the currencies of success—time, knowledge, relationships, credit, and money. It eventually shaped one of my missions to empower rehabilitation professionals and the families they serve, not just physically and functionally, but also by creating financial options for them to build their dream empire.

I leave you with this thought. In creating your empire, remember that the foundation lies within you. Uncover what D.R.I.V.Es you, harness your inherent strengths, and embrace the journey of continuous self-growth. Let's embark on this journey of creating empires, not just for the sake of personal success but for the profound impact we can make in the lives of others. Your empire awaits YOU! It is built on the pillars of your unique strengths, experiences, and an unwavering belief in your potential.

Access your Free D.R.I.V.E assessment at: https://www.discoveryourdrive.com/76119/home

CHAPTER FIFTEEN

Sunny Purcell

Sunny Purcell Real Estate / Mahana Dance Company

Entrepreneur

https://www.instagram.com/sunny.purcell/
https://www.facebook.com/sunnydpurcell/
https://www.tiktok.com/@sunny.purcell
https://www.linkedin.com/in/sunny-purcell/

Sunny Purcell is a multipreneur and public speaker based in Salt Lake City, Utah. A Los Angeles County native and graduate of the University of Southern California Marshall School of Business. Sunny owns two successful six-figure businesses: Mahana Dance Company and Sunny Purcell Real Estate. Since 2010, Mahana Dance Company has serviced over 3,000 event bookings, and Sunny Purcell Real Estate specializes in short-term rentals, showcasing her diverse entrepreneurial skills.

Sunny is a strong advocate for building careers that are both personally fulfilling and financially rewarding, a theme prevalent in her recent speaking engagements.

As the daughter of a Samoan immigrant and a devoted single parent to her daughter Eve, Sunny deeply values her heritage and family. Her hobbies include attending personal development events, spending time with family and friends, community outreach, traveling to warm climates, and being a cat mom.

Monetizing Your Passions: The Two Golden Circles

◆

By Sunny Purcell

Wrapping up my time as an undergraduate at the University of Southern California, I sat in class and excitedly daydreamed about entering the "real world." The goal was to climb the corporate ladder, wear fancy suits, and make lots of money. Soon after graduation, I was sitting in a cubicle, putting in 10-11 hour days, two-hour commutes, trapped indoors, talking to coworkers I had no real interest in, and doing work I felt nothing for. The funny thing is, I was great at what I did - operating in my "zone of excellence" as a mortgage broker, surviving two lay-offs during the 2007 housing market crash. I realized working for someone else was not for me, on the deepest level, and I soon found myself using my lunch breaks to plot my grand exit from the W-2 world over the next two years.

The story has a great ending, but the start of my entrepreneurial journey had many bumps in the road. From re-selling bulk items on eBay and rebranding my own diet supplement to a labor-intensive mobile frozen yogurt business, I was trying to figure out the business of owning your own business.

How to Monetize Your Passions

My real journey to success began once I implemented a model I call the "Two Golden Circles." This model would be the answer for the optimal success I was looking for: a) making good money on the path of least resistance and b) doing something I loved. Because the truth is, we think we cannot have it all. We think we have to sacrifice one or the other. Or both! If you neglect either, you will spend much time picking nickels off the floor or die a slow death working in an industry you care nothing about.

You may have heard the saying, 'Do what you love, and you'll never work a day in your life.' But that's not entirely true! Many leave out that there's a process of cycling through the things you love and matching them with opportunities in the market for your passion to thrive financially. The Two Golden Circles represent an empowering framework that merges your intrinsic passions with viable market opportunities. This model has not only shaped my businesses but has also steered my life, helping me navigate through both trials and triumphs.

The First Golden Circle: Discovering Your "Zone of Genius"

The concept of the "Zone of Genius" (from Gay Hendrick's "The Big Leap") is the first of the two golden circles. In this circle, write down your natural talents, deepest passions, and activities that you are good at and enjoy. For example, I **love** to dance. In my Polynesian culture, you're either a singer or a dancer. I started dancing when I was 6 but did not think I could make a living at it, so I did not seriously consider it as a career option (more on that in the next paragraph).

Launching Mahana Dance Company: Merging Passion and Business Opportunity

After identifying the items on my "Zone of Genius" list, the next step was to align it with the right business model—enter the second golden circle, the "Zone of Opportunity." This circle involves identifying possible business models, market gaps, and strong income opportunities for your passions. For example, if one of your passions is cooking, I would write down in the second golden circle a list of all the ways you know or can research how cooking is currently making money - catering from home, private chef, food truck, opening a restaurant, hosting cooking classes (virtual, online), etc. Do any of these work for you? If yes, great. If you're unsure, you can take it a step further and research existing businesses using these various business models to see how it works for them. Or if you're like me, you'll try one and course-correct as you go.

I knew I loved to dance, but that wasn't enough. I had to find a viable business opportunity. Hip-hop, pop, and other dance styles I enjoyed were an oversaturated market at the time. Instead, I decided to use my unique cultural identity to capitalize on the big Pacific Islander-themed luau and events scene in Southern California. And so, my entertainment business, Mahana Dance Company, was born.

Diversifying with Sunny Purcell Real Estate

Armed with the knowledge and success from my first venture, I circled back into real estate after a 13-year hiatus, after my soul kept calling out for me to balance out and start working my brain's left hemisphere again. However, this time, I knew I could do it in my own way versus the bland experience I had in 2007. Applying the same principles, I identified short-term rentals as a lucrative niche aligned with my joy of creating passive income, analyzing a rental's profitability potential, home design, and decor.

Overcoming Personal Challenges: Resilience Through Alignment

My journey has not been without personal challenges, from overcoming an abusive childhood to navigating life as a single parent after domestic violence relationships. These experiences have reinforced the importance of working within my "Zone of Genius," not just for financial stability but for my own sanity. Staying true to living in this manner has also provided emotional strength. Can you imagine taking on the load of healing from your past, carrying the demands of your current life, *and* working a job you despise? I cannot. And I think I would have joined the valley of depressed, anxious, morbidly obese, insecure, and codependents a long time ago.

In the toughest times, my businesses have been more than abundant income sources; they have been my rock. My wings to fly and experience more of what life has to offer, and live life more on my own terms. My pillars of resilience, standing firm, allowing me to bounce back after multiple roadblocks life threw at me. Nothing was ever that bad, and no situation was irredeemable because there was joy and light at the end of the tunnel I created for myself. One of the biggest flexes in life is to stand strong and unbothered by the clamor of haters on the rock you built yourself. It just about immediately discredits anyone when they retreat back to their 350 sq ft apartment and a job that sucks their lifeforce dry while your business makes you another $4,000 in your sleep.

Empowerment and Legacy: Living the Model

Touching on discovering one's purpose, when you're living your most authentic self via the zone of genius, the portal is open, and you receive clearer and consistent guidance on what you should be doing at any given season in your life. You are not buried in survival mode, resentment, or fear. You open the way for true alignment to happen.

The empowerment of living and working within the Two Golden Circles is profound. It has allowed me to build a life that feels authentic and purpose-driven. As I look to the future, I focus on how this model can help me continue to grow and use it to empower others, especially my daughter, Eve, and other women who see parts of their stories in mine.

By adhering to this model, I'm leaving my daughter not only a financial legacy but also a blueprint for living a fulfilled, purposeful life.

Reflecting on my journey through the Two Golden Circles, I see a path marked by bravery, alignment, challenges, and triumphs. This model has not only shaped my businesses but has also offered a framework for living. It proves that when you align what you do best with what the market needs, you don't just build a business—you build an empire.

As you chart your course, consider your own Zones of Genius and Opportunity. Where do they intersect? How can they guide your decisions? With these questions in mind, set forth and create a career and a legacy.

Remember, the most enduring empires are built on the foundations of passion and practicality—a lesson I hope to pass on through my life and work.

CHAPTER SIXTEEN

Pamela Kushlan
Multi-Passionate Entrepreneur
Payment Processing Consultant
International Lifestyle Membership Affiliate
LegalShield/IDShield Associate

linktr.ee/pamelaismypartner

I am a Multi-Passionate Entrepreneur, specializing as a: Payment Processing Consultant, International Lifestyle Membership Affiliate, LegalShield/IDShield Associate, Self-Love/Financial Freedom Activist, and Peace/Unity Seeker. I've decades of experience in Rental Properties, Office Management, Payroll, A/R, A/P, and Print Production. My favorite monikers are: Mom, Grandma, Loving Friend, Dog Mom, and Homeowner.

Inhale Truth, Exhale Trust, Embrace Change

by Pamela Kushlan

They say time is money. But for me, time is the most precious currency of all. My life has been a series of teachings in financial awareness, personal growth, valuing the potency of love, and a deep appreciation for the fleeting nature of time. It all began with a fundamental lesson: time is precious and priceless, and money is merely a tool that often dictates the quality of our life experiences. Every dollar matters, mostly because it shapes the freedom and opportunities available to help us enjoy each moment.

This truth resonated with me from a young age. Money wasn't something we took for granted growing up, as we knew it was a privilege. As kids, we seldom shopped for new clothes, as wearing hand-me-downs and mom's handmade clothes was our norm. Mom even suggested we drink powdered milk, but that was a hard pass. Eating out was a rarity for us. Some Sunday mornings were extra special when we found crumpled bills on the counter. It meant the night before, our dad had won at billiards so that Village Inn brunch may be in the cards. At my dad's 80th birthday dinner, my brother reminisced about us ironing out every dollar that had been wadded up in his pocket, making it apparent each dollar holds value.

Those Village Inn brunches also served as a practical lesson in economics. After eating, we'd guess the bill, watching the cost climb from $15 to $25. It was a fun family tradition that subtly instilled an awareness of rising costs and inflation.

Being served green sweet-and-sour spare ribs is a memory etched in our minds forever. My family will never let me live down how disgusting and awful it looked; we closed our eyes just to enjoy its taste. We teased each other often, and not only did it help us grow a thick skin, but taking ourselves too seriously was impossible. The fact is, I'd used our sugar to play with food coloring. Mom repeatedly requested that I bake cookies with that sugar, and stubbornly, I ignored her. Besides the valuable message of listening to Mom, it taught me to appreciate all I have, and if something's worth having, then it's worth making good use of it.

Playing Monopoly with Real Money was a unique monumental moment as a kid, as my parents' financial decisions had a profound impact. They refinanced our home, turning their $100 house payment into $400+ to pull $30K in equity out to purchase 3 rental homes. Not only did we discover that $15K – $20K in cash is all one needs to play, it instilled in me how valuable taking calculated risks on ourselves truly is. I saw how my parents uncomfortably stretched themselves to do this. They insisted we assist them with the rentals, so from then on, we'd clean, paint, do yard work, answer the phone for prospective tenants, etc. As time passed, it was clear that being a homeowner was wise, and leveraging it to purchase rental properties was a smart means to grow financially and was worth all of its effort.

My life's most impactful decisions were created by listening to my inner voice and acting on those prompts. At 19, my apartment's rent increased by $65/mo. Thanks to my parents' influence, I looked in the newspaper for condos for sale, making only $5.35/hr. I discovered a 2-bedroom, 1-bath condo with hookups and amenities for $27,500. While this price is a steal now, it felt very heavy then. Yet, I was impressed with its layout and location. I saw it that afternoon. That evening, I secured purchasing it by getting a $1K loan from my parents, and I financed it all within the month. I paid less monthly to own it than to rent my 1-bedroom apartment.

My world shifted when my beautiful daughter arrived 1 ½ years after getting married. At just 2 weeks old, she fell ill with a cold; she stopped breathing in my arms. The fear was paralyzing, and the next day at the ICU was a blur. Thankfully, the diagnosis was RSV, and with time, she recovered completely. This profound near-loss experience transformed me; it highlighted the importance of cherishing every moment. A few months later, we bought a home to build a secure future for our growing family; our condo became a rental property. 3 ½ years later, our family was blessed again with the arrival of a wonderful son.

My life has been a whirlwind journey - twice married, twice divorced, yet I wouldn't trade a single second. There were incredible peaks filled with love, laughter, unforgettable experiences, and the joy of growth. But valleys, too, are filled with challenges, conflict, and moments of heartbreak. Intermittently, I fell into the trap of negativity; I'd complain and blame others for my life's circumstances. However, through radical self-honesty, I found the key to saving myself. Taking accountability for my actions, my choices, my desires, and my boundaries (or lack thereof) was a turning point. I invested my time/money to gain insight from mentors/coaches. The key to my liberation and self-love was about looking at myself in the mirror to see/understand how I'd contributed to the dynamics of my life and my relationships. I learned how to honor my values, voice, and priorities, and ultimately, I rediscovered who I am and who I want to become. Looking back, I see how fear of change and a desire for comfort often held me back from reaching my full potential. I avoided my emotions and feelings rather than allow myself to feel, accept, and contemplate them. Prior to this, I wasn't being true to myself, I didn't trust myself, and I prioritized others' opinions over my own intuition. It took dedicated introspection and "inner work" to reclaim my voice, to recognize my power, to see it was me creating my life. I've since managed to sustain great friendships with my exes; I love them both.

As a reminder of this power, my mom returned a journal I wrote in as a child. Incredibly, it described the life and career path I would eventually have – a family and an office job. I was reading about my past, as I had predicted the very future I created! This experience solidified my belief in how the universe guides us, even when we resist. It validated the true capacity we have to create our reality by being intentional. It also reminded me of the importance of listening to and honoring my inner voice.

"Life is what we make of it" – my 18 yr. old daughter's tattoo. I believe the universe was talking to me through her, or she was talking directly to me ;) ... either way, I'm grateful. While at first, I was slow to grasp the potency of this statement, it resonates with me strongly now. To flourish both emotionally and financially, we must see how each of our choices, beliefs, responses, and actions directly create our reality. Time is priceless and limited; money is the tool, it's often the currency affecting the quality of our survival and what freedoms we have. To obtain a life we desire but don't yet have, it takes being open to change, being truthful with who we're being, loving all that we are, seeing all our patterns, questioning all our beliefs, becoming uncomfortable yet disciplined in shifting our priorities, and opening up to new concepts/ideas in order to play 'the money game' in life and become our best self. Sadly, schools often suggest we trade time for money – yet the wealthiest know there are many ways to accumulate riches. I wish schools taught that becoming internally rich by loving ourselves fully and being our own best friend is the highest form of wealth possible.

I feel life isn't about happiness, yet believe happiness is a choice. By accepting life happens for us, we can gain from each experience and can consciously take action to create the life of our dreams. True that we can't control every occurrence, but still, we are 100% responsible for our responses to life. Even during life's most difficult times, a silver lining likely exists if we're willing to seek it out.

In 2018, after being laid off from being an office manager for 12 ½ years, I was introduced to the fintech industry of merchant services. Though initially hesitant, I embraced this unexpected push out of my comfort zone. I saw how recurring income could improve my quality of life as my portfolio grows. Six years later, I'm thriving in this forever-evolving field; I find it rewarding to help business owners save money and streamline their payment processing as they follow their passions. I've also joined an international lifestyle membership opportunity, as I enjoy uplifting others while having the potential of multiple sources of income. As an entrepreneur, I appreciate my time flexibility and financial stability. My mindset shifted from a "money doesn't grow on trees" mentality to embracing my ability to "plant seeds" that will continue to grow and prosper.

Throughout my life, I've been deeply touched by the kindness, courage, love, and dedication of countless individuals. I've learned to embrace my intuition, even when it's frightening. In April 2024 I said yes to myself and splurged to join my parents to embark on a 22-day ocean cruise. I'm elated that I had the pleasure and privilege to join my parents on a voyage to Mexico, Hawaii, and Canada together, as it is a memory I will always treasure. I recognize the preciousness and brevity of our time together and of every moment of my life; I insist on making the most of it.

Additionally, I listened to my intuition to commit to writing this chapter of my life story, hoping it resonates with you and encourages you to be authentically honest with yourself. I believe within each of us lies a reservoir of divine wisdom, guiding us towards our fullest potential. May you learn from my experience, as I've come to see how stagnation and complacency inhibited my growth. To lead a truly fulfilling life, I feel we must continuously push beyond our comfort zones, embrace our truth, take bold, aligned action, and trust in our capacity to exceed our wildest aspirations.

This chapter concludes with introspective questions, inviting readers to reflect on their own lives:

What have you learned in recent years and months?

Are you actively growing and evolving as a person?

What are your core values?

Do you hold yourself accountable for your choices?

Are your actions aligned with your intuition?

Do you believe you deserve abundance?

By encouraging self-reflection and embracing challenges and change, this chapter aims to inspire readers to create their own "best life" story.

CHAPTER SEVENTEEN

Alexa Shaw

Yunani Life

Founder & CEO

https://yunanilife.com
https://www.facebook.com/yunanilife
https://www.instagram.com/yunanilife

Alexa Millet (Shaw) is the spirited force behind Yunani Life, a brand launched in 2023 that unites her love for natural healing and passion for empowering women. With a heart that beats for the great outdoors, Alexa is an adventurer at the core, thriving in the embrace of the wild through skiing, mountain biking, hiking, motorcycling, backpacking, and white water rafting. Her connection to nature is a sanctuary, a source of healing and authenticity. As a dedicated wife and mother, she champions balance and infuses these values into her brand, guiding others toward harmony and wellness through nature.

Alexa's career took root in 2005 as a hairstylist, where she learned the importance of truly hearing and uplifting women. She established Luxe Design in 2009, later evolving it into Luxe Design Firm in 2017. With degrees in business marketing and graphic design, her expertise spans web development, graphic design, sales, and marketing. Since 2018, as co-owner and CMO of Professional Botanicals Inc., she has united her business skills with herbal knowledge, application, and insights to foster holistic health and inspire well-being with authenticity.

The Unstoppable Journey: Manifesting Your Path

---◆---

By Alexa Shaw

Thundering down the open stretch of road, the world around me blurred into a symphony of rushing air and raw vibration of power beneath me. My hair was a wild, untamed thing. My eyes glittered, stung by the wind's embrace. My hand wrapped tightly around the throttle, easing it back to unleash a guttural cry from my motorcycle's eager heart.

To my left and right, the world was a fleeting shadow, yet, looking back in my mirror, a breathtaking sight unfolded—forty beams of headlights trailing in a glowing snake undulating over hills and valleys. We were a force of nature. Every one of us is a woman, a warrior in our own right, riding our iron horses with a roar that proclaimed our combined power.

Were the tears that traced my cheeks born of the wind's relentless onslaught, or were they a result of the inner surge of absolute empowerment? I led this band of spirited souls, each one a testament to the pure exhilaration of freedom. We were each a pillar of might, bound together, invincible, with the desert's endless canvas before us. With every mile we claimed, our sense of liberation swelled, a tangible force that fueled our journey onward that day and every day after.

This moment, this manifestation of collective strength and freedom, culminated in a journey that began with a younger version of myself. Back then, armed only with a vision and the courage to pursue it, I took a step into the unknown. That single step was the seed that would grow into this powerful sisterhood. It was the embodiment of a truth that resounded with every fiber of my being: the undeniable certainty that there is nothing women can't achieve—a conviction that had been the driving force behind my every decision and inspiration. It was a realization that everything I had been, every choice I had made, had led to not only the creation of this remarkable group but also my purpose and the woman I had grown to become.

Growing up in the rustic charm of a mountain town, my childhood was a patchwork of simple pleasures—TV binges, sugary delights, and the odd Hot Pocket. But more than anything, it's the sensation of soil underfoot that stays with me, the profound bond with the wilderness that shaped my being. The natural world was my earliest instructor, and my older brothers, though they didn't know it, were my guides. From the start, I carried a boldness within me, a silent vow that echoed, 'Anything they can do, I can do too.'

That belief meant embracing every scrape and scar, leaping from the shingles of our low-hanging roof, and weathering the tears that came with each tumble and triumph. It's why forts rose from the forest floor, grueling hikes were savored, engines dismantled and mastered, and a love affair with power tools began. From those days of dust and determination, I learned the value of toil and the art of turning problems into possibilities.

Without even realizing it, I've lived out my belief through action. At 15, I found myself confidently perched atop scaffolding, 30 feet in the air, securing the wooden siding of our family home with a nail gun in hand. By 17, I was elbow-deep in the engine of my Jeep, learning the satisfaction of a rebuild. When 19 came around, I was the proud owner of my first motorcycle, a purchase that quickly turned into a deep-seated passion. I've since logged tens of thousands of miles, guiding my bike through the rough texture of dirt roads, close encounters with wildlife, and biting, subzero storms, all while leading daring groups of women on epic, cross-border adventures.

At 27, I took on the mantle of homeownership with a historic home, embarking on a renovation that respected its rich past. I rolled up my sleeves and dove headfirst into the grime of demolition, learning to navigate the intricacies of its old-world structure, from rewiring its electrical veins to laying tile floors and uncovering a deep passion and respect for woodworking. With each experience, I learned that the so-called limits on my potential were nothing more than societal molds, ones I never fit into. Embracing this, I shattered these constructs, first as a woman defying norms and then as an entrepreneur, boldly carving my own path.

With an unwavering resolve to escape the drudgery of a typical 9-5 job, I crafted a vivid vision of self-made success. I envisioned a life where I was the master of my time, where my earnings mirrored my value, and where the necessity of travel paired seamlessly with a flourishing career. This was no simple dream but a detailed blueprint for the future. The potency of this mindset was irrefutable—a mindset so compelling it turned my visions into a lived journey.

I left behind my W-4 and boldly set sail on my entrepreneurial voyage with Luxe Design. My goal was clear: to manifest the life I had meticulously mapped out in my mind. For nearly a decade, I crafted digital artistry for thriving businesses, from websites to branding and marketing campaigns, while flourishing personally and exploring the globe. 2017 marked a significant leap forward, founding Luxe Design Firm. The new venture was both a grand stage for my ambitions and a thrilling opportunity to lead a team. However, it also meant facing the stormy seas of business ownership head-on. There were many challenges, from ensuring my team's financial security to navigating the unpredictable currents of client work.

The toughest storm hit when a major client delayed and ultimately failed to pay, dragging my firm into the depths of financial despair. This was a time of intense emotional turmoil, a period where I confronted failure face-to-face for the first time. Yet, in the aftermath of that storm, I discovered a powerful truth: it's in our moments of failure that we truly learn who we are. But from that low came a turning point. With renewed vigor, I picked myself up, dusted off, and let my mindset—the same one that had fueled my initial vision—illuminate the way forward.

I dove once again into the powerful practice of visualization to construct my future anew. A vivid picture swiftly emerged, one where I was a catalyst of empowerment for women. Radiating energy and optimism, I envisioned myself inspiring women to lead lives of fulfillment and health, unbound by societal expectations or the myth of perfection. My future was rich with meaningful dialogues on health and authentic living, and it allowed me financial freedom and precious quality time with my family. It was a life infused with the fire of movement, the tranquility of a sound bath, the introspection of meditation, and the cultivation of an abundant, balanced mindset. What single word could encompass my entire vision? Health. Physically, mentally, spiritually.

Yunani Life materialized as the culmination of my deepest dreams. Thoughtfully crafted for women, inspired by ancient natural healing practices and rooted in principles of harmony and balance. It represents not just a product but a mission to weave together physical, mental, and spiritual health, providing a platform to cultivate the community of connected, empowered, and centered women I so vividly envisioned.

Undeniable intuition told me that the universe and my subconscious were aligning to reveal this path. My being, my heritage, my experiences, and my mindset had all brought me to this moment, reaffirming my belief that women are capable of achieving anything they set their minds to. Once again, the time had come to grasp the vision with courage, to summon bravery, and to step into the unknown, emboldened by the knowledge that my future is within my power to shape.

The Manifesto for Action: Setting Goals and Speaking Them Into Existence

Manifesting your dreams into reality isn't just a matter of wishful thinking—it's about deliberate and intentional action. Here's how you can begin to turn the intangible into the tangible, step by step:

1. **Envision with Precision:** Craft a compelling visualization of your aspirations. Spare no detail in your mind's eye—envelope yourself in the sensations, emotions, and the transformed life that awaits upon their realization.
2. **Write It:** Your goals, ambitions, affirmations, and dreams onto paper. Revisit them often, letting them guide your focus, see the growth, and fortify your resolve.
3. **Speak It:** Vocalize your vision, share it with conviction, and embody it with every fiber of your being. Speak, and let the universe echo your aspirations.

Understanding why this approach matters is crucial. A clear vision is essential; by setting precise goals, you give direction to your actions and create a standard to measure your progress. Vocalizing these goals is equally important; when you talk about your ambitions, you solidify them in your mind and spur yourself into action. As you take this journey, remember that progress is made up of small, consistent steps that align with your ultimate objectives. Don't forget to celebrate your wins, no matter how small they may seem. Each one is a milestone on the path to your dream. Embrace this manifesto wholeheartedly, and through your actions, begin to shape the life you've always envisioned.

Read this, then reread it, and let this truth sink in deep: Your potential is boundless. You, a true goddess, are only confined by the boundaries of your own thoughts. It's time to shatter those barriers. Embrace the courage within you, leap into the unknown, and seize the opportunities that lay ripe for the taking. This is not just a call—it's a challenge. I personally invite you to grab a pen, a dedicated notebook, and a hot cup of coffee and let your mind start crafting. Manifest your life, and do it with a heart full of passion—RIGHT NOW. The world is waiting for your fire to ignite. This is your awakening. Go forth and become your legend.

CHAPTER EIGHTEEN

Brianna Magarrell

COO/Lifestyle Director/ Real Estate Investor

www.villaro.co
https://www.linkedin.com/in/briannamagarrell07/
https://www.instagram.com/bri_darby/
https://www.facebook.com/brianna.magarrell/

Like a lotus flower rising from the mud to blossom into beauty, I see myself as a beacon of strength and positivity. Despite various hardships, I've grown as a resilient force, determined to make a difference. As a Lifestyle Director, I excel in fostering community engagement, using my intuitive understanding of people to unite them. Beyond my profession, I am a real estate investor, advocating for alternative income streams to help avoid putting a cap on life. Surrounded by cherished family and friends, I embrace every opportunity to uplift and encourage those around me. My life's journey reflects the lotus flower's resilience and beauty, reminding others that no matter their challenges, they rise above and find their version of a lotus flower, too. Life knows no bounds, and everyone has the power to shape their life.

My Journey of Strength and Forgiveness

By Brianna Magarrell

Life wasn't a fairytale for me. It wasn't a walk through a rose garden but a trek through a swamp – murky, unpredictable, and sometimes the hardest journey. Yet, like a lotus flower pushing through the muck to bloom into beauty, I found my strength and resilience, which helped form me into the person I am today.

My childhood was a confusing combination of love and struggle. My parents, though they gave us everything we ever wanted, were locked in a constant struggle. Dad, a Navy SEAL, was a trained soldier with dark memories. One day, my dad was gone; he was not part of our life like he was. The details are still fuzzy, but I remember many visits to a sterile building with high fences and even Christmases with Santa in that same building. Once I was old enough to know, the truth was brutal. My dad, the man sworn to protect, tried to take my mom's life. Twice. The first time was with his own hands; the second time, he hired someone. This is when my mom signed me up for Gymnastics; this became my refuge, a sanctuary of structure and discipline. In the world of hard work and dedication, I found focus and a sense of control even with the chaos at home.

As the truth about Dad's actions became more known to me, I wanted nothing to do with him. Mom, scared from what had happened, found comfort or numbness in alcohol. My childhood was beautiful and wonderful, but as I was older, and at this point, my dad was out of prison, it became more of a tiptoe around her moods and anxieties from my dad. But even though she always had the fear of my dad in her mind, there were plenty of moments of pure love, laughter, and endless memories that she helped create. Mom, a single parent juggling two kids and a full-time job, never let that get in the way of our childhood until drinking became more common.

College was my escape hatch, a chance to become an adult and create my own habits, finances, and means to pay bills. Although I needed help with bills and didn't want to burden my mom with more expenses, I reached out to my dad for the first time in a long time to help me with college. The distance was still big between us; I was hesitant to start that relationship with him, but a new life bloomed – my beautiful baby sister from my Dad helped rekindle a relationship with him so I could be in my little sister's life.

Graduation came, a significant achievement in life. I invited my dad to share that memory with me because he had missed so many of my achievements before. This was supposed to be an exciting day for me. But the memories of the past still bring fear to my Mom. To shield Mom from seeing Dad, I orchestrated a covert mission, an attempt to have everyone there to see me walk those steps. This day became more about my Mom and my family, putting stress on me that I created this issue for my Mom, and I shouldn't be putting my Mom through this. I felt that this day was about me and that what she didn't know wouldn't hurt her.

I moved back home, and I noticed that the alcohol, her crutch for many years, became worse. Watching her decline, I reached my breaking point. The "straightforward and honest" girl I finally blew! I gave her a heart-wrenching ultimatum – rehab, or she was no longer my mom. I was done coming home wondering if she was still breathing or declining a night out with my friends to go home and make sure she got something in her stomach besides liquor.

The hospital became the battleground where we fought for my mom's future. The sight of her fragile and yellow body was a gut punch. Watching her struggle to take the paper wrapper off the plastic straw is one of my strongest memories to this day. This was when a battle between myself and my family came into place, and I poured my heart out about rehab. My family insisted this wasn't the right time to discuss it, but look where we are. This is the exact time to talk about this.

Rehab wasn't sunshine and rainbows. It was a big realization that this was not where she belonged; this was not the life my mom was meant to have. My mom finally faced her horrifying past, and slowly, the Mom I remembered came back. Her skin was back to its regular color, her hair grew thicker, and she was happy again.

Today, our family represents strength and forgiveness. Though geographically distant, Dad has built a dream life in Tennessee with my little sister, his wife, and grandkids. Radiant and healthy, Mom is living her best life, finally free from dwelling on the past and seeing the world with her other half. As for me, I've learned an important lesson: life is a journey of self-discovery, not a puzzle waiting to be solved.

Now that I have shared my story of how I became stronger and learned to forgive, I wouldn't be complete without sharing the tools that helped me become stronger and learn to forgive. The amazing women in my life, especially my mom, instilled these values in me. She always taught me the importance of kindness and how lending a helping hand can make a difference. I believe this kindness is a foundation for strength and forgiveness. These are the steps that I have taken that made me a stronger person and developed the skills to learn to forgive.

Become Stronger:

Identify your inner strength: We all have it. What experiences have made you resilient? What are you passionate about? Reflect on these and build upon them. For me, remembering my passions and what I've overcome helped build my foundation. My grandmother also played a significant role. Her independence and self-reliance instilled a strong sense of self in me, which has proven to be a source of strength throughout my life.

Challenge yourself: When you are comfortable, that is a red flag. Step outside your comfort zone. Challenge yourself! Taking a class, learning a new skill, or even facing a small fear can be a confidence booster. I found that even something simple, like making my bed every day, was a powerful first step.

Embrace Setbacks. They are inevitable. View them as lessons, not failures. Instead of asking, "Why did this happen to me?" I try to ask, "Why did this happen to me?". This shift in perspective helps me adapt and keep moving forward.

Build a Support System. Surround yourself with positive, encouraging people who believe in you. Remember, as they say, "The only true wealth is the wealth of your relationships." These connections uplift and inspire you, just like mine have for me.

Practice Self-Care. It's not selfish, it's essential! Eat healthy, exercise, and find healthy ways to manage stress. Taking care of yourself fuels your strength and resilience!

Learn to Forgive:

Acknowledge Your Hurt. Don't bottle it up. Allow yourself to feel the emotions, but don't dwell on them.

Understand, Not Condone: My grandfather's advice stuck with me: "Imagine sitting next to someone to understand them rather than across from them." Trying to see things from the other person's perspective, even if it's difficult, can foster empathy and release negativity.

Release the Resentment: Holding onto anger hurts you more than anyone. Forgive for your own peace, not for the other person. Dwelling on the past only holds you back. As I learned through forgiving my parents, I use those memories to build on future experiences.

Set Boundaries: Forgiveness doesn't mean trusting someone who betrayed you. Protect yourself from further harm, but learn from the past. There's a time to walk away, and being the bigger person is okay. As my dad used to say, 'Help someone pull their wagon to the next destination. If they get in the wagon and expect you to pull it on your own, then stop.' This emphasizes the importance of offering help but also knowing when to disengage from unhealthy dynamics.

Practice Self-Compassion: Forgive yourself too. We all make mistakes. Learn and move on and learn from them.

Remember, incredible strength and forgiveness are within you. Believe in yourself, and never stop growing. Embrace challenges, nurture your support system, and prioritize self-care. Most importantly, remember the power you hold to inspire others. Sharing my story is not just about me; it's about showing my younger siblings and anyone who might be reading that strength and forgiveness are possible. I strive to be a positive influence, someone they can look up to and emulate. It's about rising above the murky waters, blooming with strength, and finding your own inner light. And just like the lotus flower, we all have the blossoming flower. It's waiting to be discovered, nurtured, and shared.

CHAPTER NINETEEN

Rossina Lake

RC2 Communications

CEO

RC2comm.net
https://linktr.ee/rossina_lake
https://linktr.ee/rc2_communications

Rossina is the founder and CEO of RC2 Communications, a multicultural agency focused on brand and cultural integration. She is a distinguished marketing and advertising professional with over two decades of experience encompassing business development, account management, public relations, and government communications. Her dedication to fostering collaboration among diverse groups has established her as a key connector within Utah's communities.

With a multicultural background and expertise in both the private and government sectors, Rossina possesses a unique ability to engage with diverse cultures and spearhead grassroots marketing and advertising initiatives. Throughout her career, she has contributed to numerous local and national campaigns, including significant projects during her tenure at Univision Communications and her current agency. She later expanded her communications expertise to the government sector, serving as the Spanish Public Information Officer for the State of Utah COVID-19 Response and as the Public Information Officer for the Utah Governor's Office.

Rossina holds a Bachelor's degree in Marketing and International Business. She is a fervent advocate for small business entrepreneurs, women's empowerment, and health issues.

Currently, Rossina serves on the Advisory Board for KUER 90.1 FM and the Steering Committee for KUUB 88.3 FM, the nation's first bilingual public radio station. Previously, she served as a member of the Executive Committee of the Board of Directors for The Suazo Business Center, a non-profit dedicated to aiding multicultural entrepreneurs. She also chaired the Go Red Por Tu Corazon Leadership Committee of the American Heart Association, promoting health awareness among women, and was a founding member of Soroptimist International Latinas of Salt Lake, which supports women's education.

The Woven Threads of Life

◆

By Rossina Lake

Life is a rich tapestry, woven with threads of experiences, cultures, and personal journeys...Asi es Mi Vida.

My name is Rossina, derived from the ancient word for 'rose,' symbolizing beauty and complexity with each petal unfolding stories not immediately seen by the eye. My journey has been one that embraces my origins while pursuing new dreams by connecting with diverse cultures and backgrounds but always holding strong to the values that define me. Creating a kind and empathetic environment that respects everyone's uniqueness is like weaving a beautiful tapestry, where each distinct thread contributes to the overall masterpiece.

My roots are deeply embedded in my beloved Honduras, where I was nurtured by a loving, large extended family that instilled traditional values, emphasizing kindness and consideration. The divorce of my parents marked my childhood, leaving me and my sister to navigate the complexities of communication and family dynamics. We learned the arts of negotiation and peacekeeping early on, a necessity for maintaining harmony. These skills proved very useful later as I built relationships and partnerships in my future professional pursuits.

During my teenage years, I frequently traveled to the United States as an opportunity to visit family and practice my English. I am grateful for my parents, who cared about providing a good bilingual education. My mom always made us prioritize our academic goals and dreams. After graduating from High School, I pursued studying Fashion Design abroad. My passion for design started early. I was sketching and dreaming of becoming a fashion designer. I also enjoyed renewing vintage clothes, accessories, and shoes! I often designed for my closest friends for parties, events, and sixth-grade and high-school graduations, among others. I was constantly updating my portfolio and sharing my designs with whoever wanted to take them to the seamstress. We all had one back home; it was part of our culture, and by creating my clothes, I learned the importance of a meticulous, perfectionist eye. Creating my own clothes deepened my understanding of artistic design and attention to detail—skills that seamlessly transitioned into my marketing career. It was during this creative and formative time in my life that I met my future husband in Utah. After reconnecting seven years later, we married and have since built a life together over the past 21 years, raising two remarkable sons.

Over time, my career path transitioned from fashion sketches to marketing strategies—a shift driven by my father's pragmatic views. As a hard-working, conservative lawyer, he guided me toward a career that promised stability. Thus, I ventured into marketing and international business, a path that aligned with my personality and broadened my perspectives on life. It was through marketing that I found a way to weave my creative passions with practical applications and insights, leading to early involvement in agricultural exports. Later, when I moved to the US, it eventually led me to play a crucial role in joining the team developing a Spanish language network in Utah. This experience taught me that business growth thrives on understanding and tapping into new audiences by connecting the community with cultural, healthcare, and educational resources. I developed the skill to recognize the needs of our community as it became the nation's fastest-growing minority market. Recognizing the opportunity to address these needs, I founded my own multicultural marketing and advertising consulting firm. My agency was crucial in enabling me to work with a dedicated team of communicators during the historic pandemic, focusing on the state's well-being. This collaboration ultimately led to my service in the state

I cherish and call home, and subsequently, working at the magnificent Utah State Capitol.

For me, every venture was not only about business growth but about fostering understanding and empathy across diverse cultures. Throughout my journey, I have been blessed to live the ups and downs of my story with strength, grit, and resilience. Rising from challenges and celebrating the open doors and opportunities, as well as the ones that have closed to shape who I am today. A defining experience for me was assisting in building a local Spanish network in a conservative market where we represented a small minority of the population at that time. It took planning, prospecting, market outreach, constant client follow up and delivery, focusing on how to increase their presence and their revenue. This challenge not only taught me the immense value of working within a diverse team, but it also equipped me with the ability to adapt and rebuild, ensuring that I can navigate and thrive in varied and challenging environments. I learned how to engage with the mainstream market by sharing messages of empathy and value, which helped dismantle stereotypes and encourage acceptance of new cultures. My mission has been to advocate for the integration of the minority and mainstream markets by encouraging open conversations that cultivate understanding. As a business owner in my community, I am dedicated to providing services that not only improve branding and recognition but also give clients valuable insights and experiences from engaging with different cultures.

In every role I've taken, I have strived to create a safe environment based on strong collaboration among partners, where creative and positive interactions flourish. This commitment to fostering inclusive, empathetic relations has been a cornerstone of my professional life and continues to guide how I work and interact with others.

The most profound test of my strength came in the most unexpected way I could have thought—one of those situations in which you never expect to touch your family. My athletic and strong son was cowardly sucker punched in the back of the head after basketball practice in the locker room by a teammate because my son refused to fight him and turned his back on him. We almost lost our son due to this incident that ultimately could have been avoided and was due to a moment of anger. Our lives were crushed. It was before the pandemic lockdown, but we were already isolated, so the lockdown did not impact us much. It actually became a blessing in disguise; we were able to focus on our son's rehab, six to nine hours of daily therapy between different healthcare institutions. We did this for five consecutive months after seven weeks of inpatient rehab. That's what our lives became. From day one, I could only bring out my warrior mom self, tapping into an internal and unexplainable force that only a mom has to stand strong and hold the fort with prayer, resilience, and faith when no one else can. Our son had to relearn to walk, eat, talk, and be himself again. He is a tremendous inspiration to me; his heart, discipline, and determination are like no other. He is a warrior. I am grateful every day for seeing him continue his life, overcoming all obstacles and stigmas that society imposes on an injured athlete. Throughout this ordeal, we persevered, integrating as much as we could into our daily routine to keep both our lives and our business moving forward despite the emotional distress that this incident instilled in each of us. As a family, we survived and emerged stronger, our bonds fortified by adversity. This traumatic experience, while scarring, taught us the impermanence of security and the undeniable presence of a higher grace guiding us through life's tumultuous waters.

In inexplicable ways, God knows when changes need to happen in your journey and when He will open a new path to heal, strengthen, and recharge you. The right time will come to you and you have to be prepared to embrace it, even if it comes in a way you didn't plan it. Learn to enjoy the moment and breathe new air.

Today, as I reflect on my journey, I am grateful for the power of perseverance, the beauty of diversity, and the strength of authentic connection. Each experience, each challenge, and each triumph is a thread in the ever-expanding tapestry of my life. I continue with the same commitment to advocacy that marked my beginnings while applying the lessons and insights I've gained to leverage my client's outreach strategies. It is a joy to collaborate with the ones who recognize the value of embracing diverse communities and how differences can foster a rich ecosystem for the newer generations. As I integrate the fascinating diversity and nuances that new audiences represent, I see an evolution that will continue expanding into a more vibrant, multilingual world. Our world is indeed a bright one, with all the uniqueness of each different and individual thread that is woven into the beautiful tapestry of life.

In sharing my story, I hope to inspire others to embrace their unique backgrounds, to face life's challenges with courage, and to always find joy in the journey. For in this complex, beautiful tapestry of life, each of us is crucial in enriching the world, weaving together a legacy of empathy, strength, and unity for generations to come.

The best opportunity you can give yourself—is to live authentically, passionately, and empathetically, nurturing a world where every individual's story is valued, every culture is celebrated, and every challenge is met with resilience and hope.

CHAPTER TWENTY

Nathalie Herrey

Queen's Gambit LLC

Boss lady & CEO

Nathalie Herrey
@realnathalieherrey

Nathalie Herrey has had the opportunity to experience life in ways few can imagine - from excruciating hardship to finding joy!

Today, she lives her passion with a clear mission of helping others know that they can conquer anything life throws at them and claim their Crown. Life is meant to be lived with purpose, joy, and fulfillment.

With her degrees in Psychology and Leadership & Management, as well as decades as a corporate consultant, working with Tony Robbins, Dean Graziosi, Jay Shetty, etc., she has a passion for empowering men and women through servant leadership. Providing them with tools and guidance for life and careers, helping them find and live their superpowers.

She is a multiple Amazon bestseller, international speaker, and entrepreneur.

Her greatest achievement in life are her four children. She currently resides in Salt Lake City, with her 4 children and 3 dogs.

It is time to #StepIntoTheArena of your Life - it is time to #PickUpYourCrown 👑 ✨

Your Empire Within

◆

By Nathalie Herrey

"You must always have faith in people. And most importantly, you must always have faith in yourself." —Elle Woods.

Get comfortable with being unrelatable and uncomfortable, and you will travel this journey and create your empire with much more ease.

When I was nine years old, I sat on the couch in my house, watching my uncles win the largest music competition in the world - 50,000 screaming fans in the audience - and 1 billion viewers watching over television and joining the ranks of musicians like ABBA and Céline Dion.

A few months earlier, they had won the qualifying competition in Sweden, and I was so excited! I was so happy that all of their hard work had come to fruition, and all of Sweden was celebrating with them!

Now, watching my uncles win the entire competition in Luxembourg, tears started running down my face. This was a lot for a nine-year-old girl who had been living a pretty ordinary life until then. Two of my uncles lived in the basement of my family's house at the time, and we already had fans sitting day and night outside our home, filling up the driveway, hoping for any sight or sound from my uncles. I knew I had seen nothing yet.

That same year, my father, who also became the manager for my uncles, won an Olympic medal in Los Angeles. To say that it was a successful year for my family is an understatement. It was a whirlwind of stadium concerts, travels, excited fans, and the opportunity to meet many people.

I remember after one of the concerts, we went to the house of a young girl who had been trampled when they opened up the door to the stadium, and she had broken her arm in the chaos. It taught me about compassion, seeing even the smallest of us, and always giving kindness and value.

When I was about 12, my father competed in the world championships in Rome. I remember the heat being so excruciating. My father had 50 km, longer than a marathon, to race that day. His sport is judged by live judges, and if you get three red warnings, you are disqualified from continuing the competition. My father had two red warnings and one-third of the race left to go.

I had spent countless hours on my bike next to my dad as he trained relentlessly. Sometimes, I traveled in the backseat of a car because it was too hot or too far that day for me to use the bike. I watched my dad fall back from being in the front of the pack to almost the very back. My heart broke for him. I ran along the fenced-off track and yelled at him, "Don't give up, Pappa! It's not over yet!"

There must have been so much going on in his head, and his body must have been in so much pain at this point of the race, but somehow, he heard me, and slowly but surely, he started gaining on his fellow competitors again. He was in third place when he walked into that stadium to finish that race. I've never forgotten how I felt that day. It Solidified a bond with my dad that will never go away.

It taught me the power of having someone cheer you on, even if sometimes it's only you cheering for yourself, and the power of the mind when you decide it's not over yet!

I'm sure it sounds amazing, and I feel blessed to have grown up in a family with high achievers, but it also came with a tremendously high price. Fame brought incredible dysfunction to my family, and I had to grow up quickly and shoulder unique emotional and physical responsibilities.

It taught me some valuable lessons that I have carried with me ever since;

Every single person matters. It doesn't matter if you're the janitor scrubbing the toilets or a famous businessman or rockstar. We all deserve to be seen and be found valuable for the simple fact that we are sharing this life as human beings together.

Any example in your life, whether good or bad, is an example from which you can draw guidance. If you grow up in a family that's very dysfunctional, or you have been neglected or abused, you know with clarity how that feels. Hopefully, you will treat others the opposite because you don't want anyone to feel how you felt or treated the way you were treated.

But most of all, I have realized that if we can stop being shocked by life's difficulties, we can work through those times much faster and with a stronger heart.

Life is going to be uncomfortable. That is not necessarily a bad thing. We know that to grow a muscle, we have to go through uncomfortable resistance for it to do so. Life is the same way. When we can start to relax and feel uncomfortable, we will be able to have the opportunity to unleash the potential within us that otherwise would be kept at bay.

So, diving into adulthood is so fun—right?* Please insert a hint of sarcasm. Those wild childhood experiences weren't just memories but a roadmap for my entrepreneurial journey. Watching my family conquer the world in music and sports? That leaves a mark.

But as you know, being an entrepreneur isn't waking up one day and deciding to be a boss. No, for me, it was out of necessity; I was out of options, and coming out of COVID, there was no other option.

I didn't have it all figured out from the get-go—and I still don't. Entrepreneurship is like navigating a maze blindfolded—you stumble, you fall, but you keep moving forward because what else will you do? As a single mother with no partner or family to help, I knew I had to keep going no matter what for my children.

Sure, there were bumps along the road, mainly regarding my romantic relationships. I have wanted love and family, but it has remained elusive. I have paid a very high price for those failures, but I have been blessed with four absolutely incredible children. Whatever I will not be able to accomplish in my lifetime, they will be in theirs. Every setback in life, whether personal or professional, was a test of resilience and problem-solving. I would either learn to roll with the punches or get knocked out, simple as that. Getting knocked out has never been an option for me.

Failure. I've had my fair share, for sure. But as Thomas Edison said about inventing the light bulb, "I have not failed. I've just found 10,000 ways that won't work." Don't I know it! But I have been lucky to have a tribe of amazing friends, mentors, and guides. People who had held me up when it seemed too much inspired me and believed in me and my crazy ideas so I could make them a reality.

Genuine authenticity? That was non-negotiable. I wasn't about to sell out or compromise my values of authenticity. My life goal is to leave others knowing they are valuable to me. I have stayed true to myself, believing in taking the higher road, even when it would've been easier to blend in or retaliate.

So, here it is: entrepreneurship is not for the faint of heart. It's messy and unpredictable, but it is so rewarding. When you're building your empire, you're not just chasing success—you're chasing your dreams.

And yes, it's going to be uncomfortable. You will doubt yourself and second-guess every decision, but that's all part of the journey. In those moments of discomfort, you grow the most and discover what you're truly capable of. Don't run from that. Lean into it.

If we want to join the top 2%, the change-makers and reverse engineers, we will feel unrelatable to the people around us. Building your own empire, whatever that looks like to you, will require you to act and live in a way most others are unwilling to. It is a different mindset. It is a different approach to life.

So, to all the Queens and Kings, dreamers, and rebels out there, I say this: Embrace the chaos, lean into the uncertainty, and never, ever give up. The world needs more people who are crazy enough to believe they can change it. So pick up your crown. It is waiting for you.

CHAPTER TWENTY-ONE

Angie Hewett

Your Proven Home Solution

President and Owner

https://www.saltlakecityhomebuyers.com/
https://linktr.ee/angiehewett

Angie Hewett is a multifaceted individual, excelling as both a real estate investor and an accomplished business owner. In addition to her professional achievements, she cherishes her roles as a devoted wife and beloved grandmother, finding profound joy in family bonds. Angie's diverse interests extend to mastering forgotten skills like the art of baking sourdough bread, crafting handmade soaps and lotions, and nurturing her flourishing garden. Her proficiency in these traditional crafts reflects her passion for preserving heritage practices and embracing a rich, fulfilling life. Her dedication to both personal and professional endeavors illuminates her vibrant spirit and unwavering dedication to a meaningful life.

Embracing Change: Redefining Success After a Setback

by Angie Hewett

The day the Zoom call popped up on my screen during my usual quiet lunch break, I knew something was off. My stomach lurched as I saw my boss's face alongside the face of the HR representative. It was like being hit by a rogue wave – a rush of uncertainty and dread washing over me.

My dear boss, a man I truly respected, struggled to maintain his composure as he delivered the news. Layoffs. Over a hundred of us, me included. The HR rep, on the other hand, was all business, rattling off details with practiced efficiency.

At that moment, a myriad of emotions and disjointed thoughts flooded my mind: devastation, confusion, fear, even a sliver of relief. Silly thoughts ranged from "Can I afford my hair appointment scheduled for that evening?" to heavy ones like "Why me? What about me made me not worth keeping?" Over the next few days and weeks, feelings of great sadness and despair filled my soul, causing me to question my value and my very worth.

Along with losing my job, I had also lost my "work family," I had worked alongside amazing people for years, and we had developed a close-knit team who had been there for each other through new babies, divorce, illnesses, and even tackling home repairs via Zoom! The loss was two-fold, and I felt isolated. But isolated, I was not! Headlines from the first quarter of 2023 announced dozens of tech companies were laying off people, from Microsoft to Google and many more. Estimates were that over two hundred and fifty thousand people in my industry were laid off.

So, what is anyone to do after a job loss? Start searching for another – right when you are at your most vulnerable. Writing a resume while questioning your worth is a monumental task. Did anything you did matter? Would a new employer think it was important? How would I differentiate myself from the quarter of a million other job seekers in the technology field?

Then came the rejection letters—the "not at this time" emails and the "thank you for your application…" emails. They were piling up, and I dreaded checking my email.

The following days were a blur. The weight of insecurity pressed down on me, questioning my worth. Why me? Had I somehow fallen short? Losing my job felt like losing a part of myself, shaking the very foundation of my core.

However, amid this turmoil, I knew I wanted something that wouldn't leave me vulnerable to the whims of others or the markets and would put me in the driver's seat and allow me to direct my future. I didn't want another employer dashing my hopes or in control of how much money I could make or if I could make it tomorrow. I wanted independence to design my future, so I started looking at opportunities. After much soul searching and prayer, I followed my passion and started a real estate investing firm.

I had been thinking about this for years, but due to the "golden handcuffs," I had not had the freedom to pursue this dream. Now, with this unexpected freedom thrust upon me, I could pursue this dream.

Thankfully, my new husband and loved ones were my unwavering support system as I explored the possibility of starting my own real estate investment business. It was a daunting proposition, a tightrope walk between risk and reward. Yet, the promise of fulfillment and autonomy was intoxicating.

Starting a new business is exciting and uncomfortable. There were and still are times when I questioned my decision. Sometimes, I felt fake, the dreaded imposter syndrome. Other times, I felt like hiding or giving up, and during those times, I focused on why I was doing this.

Many challenges to starting a business need to be addressed and handled to drive oneself to success. Many of them are focused on mindset and not on the activities related to starting the business. They include managing time and focus, learning the ins and outs of my new industry, and facing multiple fears.

I am the busiest person; I go from dawn's first rays to late at night, but when I look at my priorities and desired outcomes, I do not make progress. I'd tell myself, it's okay, you can tackle it tomorrow, only to find myself at the end of another day (or week) wondering why I didn't do what I knew I needed to do.

Then, there were all the distractions, but not ones that would help me grow my business. Looking back, the more intensely I felt pressure to "do" something in the business, the greater and more numerous the distractions were. I had to learn methods to focus my mind and avoid procrastination. I still struggle with this today, but I am quicker at recognizing and changing my behavior.

There were also questions about "How to." I learned how to structure an offer, talk to homeowners and get them to accept my offers, get financing, estimate repairs, address tax and legal concerns, and so on. Fortunately, I could find resources and connect with people willing to help.

Finally, I had to face my fears. Fear of failure and success, fear of knocking on a door or picking up a phone, etc. I often drove to the home of a distressed homeowner and parked down the street to scope out the house. I'd wonder if there was someone home. Should I knock? Maybe I should just leave a door hanger. Then I'd rush to the door and place a door hanger and the next day berate myself for not knocking – for heaven's sake, I'd HAVE to speak to the homeowner if I ever wanted to get this business going.

Another fear was broadcasting my choice on social media. People I respected in the business were very vocal about what they were doing on social media. Yet part of me was afraid that if I didn't make it in this new business venture, I'd have to return to a "job." I didn't want a future employer to scope me out on social media and disregard me as a potential employee because I had a business that might distract me from a job working for them. I also feared opening up and being vulnerable on social media; what if I failed – the whole world would see it? On top of it all was the feeling of being fake; how could I tell a homeowner that I had the solution to their problem and could help – if I've never done it before? I don't think that someone would feel comfortable if I were to say, "I think I can help you, but I'm not exactly sure how or 100% confident that it will happen." Can you imagine their response?

Then, finally, the why? Why was I embarking on this journey? Was it just because the headlines announced more layoffs daily, or were the rejection letters piling up? Was I just doing this because I was not having success with the job hunt? Why did I want to start a new business? Was it just about chasing personal ambitions? Making money? Being the CEO of my own company?

No, it was about making a difference in me, my life, and the lives of my loved ones. I had a perfect example - my elderly parents. They were living in a crumbling house, their retirement dreams suffocated by mounting repair costs, their desires to travel, to see kids and grandkids denied because of the millstone of a house around their necks. They struggled on a limited income and could not escape the situation. I realized this was my chance to help them, and countless others, escape similar nightmares.

The deeper I delved into the world of real estate investing, the more inspired I became. It wasn't just about turning a profit; it was about helping others, building vibrant communities, revitalizing neglected neighborhoods, and empowering people to take action to solve their problems.

Staying focused on my purpose my why, has helped me start this business and create the foundation to build my empire. I still have a journey in front of me, but I continue to focus on my whys, share my story, connect with others, and embrace the challenges. It isn't easy, but it is worth it.

The layoff, however brutal, became the catalyst for my change. The "golden handcuffs" were broken, replaced by the freedom to create a new future for me and my loved ones. The fear of vulnerability transformed into a determination to share my knowledge and expertise with others. Please feel free to contact me using the information listed at the beginning of this chapter.

Here are a few things for you to reflect on about your journey:

1. Identify Your Own "Golden Handcuffs."

- Reflect on your career. Are you in a comfortable but unfulfilling job? Is there an opportunity you are excited about?
- Are things holding you back from pursuing a more passionate path?
    - Of change, financial security, or simply not knowing where to start.

2. Find Your Spark:
- Identify a spark that could ignite a new passion or career path.
  - Do you have a specific interest, a hidden talent, or a desire for a more meaningful life?

3. Conquer Your Vulnerability:
- Do you have something in your life that requires vulnerability, whether it is starting a business, pursuing a creative dream, or simply putting yourself out there socially?
  - Brainstorm ways to overcome this fear and embrace the power of vulnerability.

4. Building Your Dream:
- Have you set achievable goals, developed a timeline, or identified needed resources?

5. Share Your Story:
- Share your journey of overcoming challenges and pursuing your dreams.
  - Share through social media, writing a blog post, or simply having a conversation with a friend or family member.
- Sharing stories creates a sense of community and can inspire others to take their leap of faith. Share!

Made in the USA
Middletown, DE
14 July 2024